Information strategy in practice

Liz Orna has done it again! The well-known author of *Practical Information Policies* has followed up that seminal book with another one. The title of the book says it all. Mixing fascinating and insightful lessons learned from her own consultancy experience with references to the key authors in the field, she provides a step-by-step approach to developing and implementing successful information strategies in organizations, whilst at the same time highlighting how information management and knowledge management complement each other. Supported by excellent graphics, this book will be invaluable to all information managers and students of information management.

Professor Charles Oppenheim
Dept of Information Science, Loughborough University

Have you ever felt confused by the abstruse language of information and knowledge management gurus? Have you ever felt uncertain before the all too brilliant cases intended to prove their points? Have you ever felt helpless when trying to figure out how to apply their bright ideas? Whether your answer is yes or no, this book is for you if you seriously want to understand or apply strategic information management. Because Elizabeth Orna provides you with the most comprehensive yet concise, articulate and practical view of this somewhat complex activity.

Would you believe that she begins with definitions for the basic concepts and sticks to them? The next chapters take the reader smoothly through the logical paths of designing and implementing an information strategy. Some of the chapters are reproduced from her *Practical Information Policies* (1999), and, in this new book, she has added to each of them an extensive 'how to do it' section grounded in real-life experience. These additional insights should encourage readers of the earlier work to renew their acquaintance through this unique new book.

Extensive use of tables and graphic representations also contributes to making the contents more readily accessible. The last two chapters offer a challenging review of the underlying conceptual framework and good advice on how to overcome common obstacles. This book adds to recognized wisdom on the subject a special touch that will help practitioners and scholars to make good sense of it. A praiseworthy contribution.

Michel J. Menou
Visiting Professor of Information Policy, Dept of Information Science,
City University, London

D0217994

Elizabeth Orna

Information strategy in practice

GOWER

Published by
Gower Publishing Limited
Gower House
Croft Road
Aldershot
Hants GU11 3HR
England

Gower Publishing Company
Suite 420
101 Cherry Street
Burlington, VT 05401-4405 USA

Elizabeth Orna has asserted her right under the
Copyright, Designs and Patents Act 1988 to be
identified as the author of this work.

British Library
Cataloguing in Publication Data
Orna, Elizabeth
    Information strategy in practice
    1. Information resources management
    2. Strategic planning
    I. Title
658.4'038

Library of Congress Control Number: 2003056884

ISBN 0 566 08579 8

Design, typesetting, page make-up and drawings
by Graham Stevens.

Typesetting and page make-up in QuarkXPress;
drawings in Freehand; text typeface: Underware
Dolly, designed in 2001, and Linotype Avenir,
designed in 1988 by Adrian Frutiger.

Printed and bound in Great Britain by
MPG Books Limited, Bodmin.

Contents

Acknowledgements

This book is based on experience of the fascinating world of organizations and their attempts to make sense of information. That experience owes much to people with whom I have worked in various contexts, who have contributed greatly to my understanding. It is a pleasure to acknowledge the debt, while accepting sole responsibility for whatever shortcomings they have failed to rescue me from.

The first acknowledgement should go to the anonymous organization in which the recent information audit described in the book was carried out, and the audit team there, for their generous permission to draw on the documents produced during the audit. I know how great is the demand for such actual examples of doing the job in real life, and greatly appreciate their willingness to make them available.

I am grateful to Professor Don Marchand of IMD International, Lausanne for permission to quote extensively from *Information Orientation* by himself and colleagues, and for reading and commenting on drafts; to Professor Charles Oppenheim and Joan Stenson of Loughborough University for permission to quote from their research reports on valuing information assets, and for reading drafts; and to Judith Sweetman for drawing my attention to Essex County Council's post of Corporate Information Sharing and Information Security (ISIS) Manager, and to the Council for permission to quote from the responsibilities of the job, and to reproduce Figures 2.3 and 2.4.

I am indebted to Kevin Miles who brought the story of Surrey Police, quoted in Chapter 7, up to date and provided a memorable quotation; to Simon Grant of Tate, for permission to draw on a case study carried out there during my doctoral research; to many colleagues from whom I have learned in the course of shared work and discussions; and to various institutions and organizations for the opportunity to offer the ideas which appear in this book to a variety of audiences, in particular:
– Queensland University of Technology and the University of Technology Sydney where colleagues invited me to run workshops for their students in 2002
– Aslib for the opportunity of running information audit courses over a number of years
– Aslib KIMNET (lately the Information Resources Management Network) for providing a forum to test ideas and learn from colleagues in a friendly environment
– The Knowledge Management Interest group of the OGC e-Foundation for an opportunity to present the ideas on taxonomy set out in Chapter 7. The people taking part in forums like these put their own thoughts and experience into the exchanges with great generosity, and I am glad to take this opportunity of thanking everyone who has done so.

I am grateful to Suzie Duke of Gower for her unfailing support and pertinent comments, and particularly for inviting me to write this book. It has given me the chance to produce something for an audience which is dear to my heart.

Finally, my thanks to Graham Stevens, who, over a period of more than 20 years, has designed every book I've written, and has found creative and elegant solutions to every design problem that my writing, and miscellaneous external constraints, have put in his way.

Before we begin ...

It may ... be best to follow the advice of the philosopher Karl Popper and,
realising the sterility of arguments about the meanings of words, explain
our understanding of terms, rather than attempting to convince others
that our definitions are 'correct'
–BAWDEN, D. (2001)

These are the definitions which I use for the main concepts in this book – it seems right, as recommended in the above quotation, to explain my 'understanding of terms' at the start. Some of the definitions will appear again later, in extended form, but I hope it will be useful to have them here for easy reference, as well as for reflection before starting to read the book.

Knowledge

Knowledge is what we acquire from our interaction with the world; it is the results of experience organized and stored inside each individual's own mind in a way that is unique to each (though there are features common to how we all do this). It comes in two main kinds: knowledge about things, and know-how, and our knowledge is available to us at various levels from 'tacit' – what we know and use without expressing it in words, to 'explicit' – what we can readily formulate and explain (for more about tacit knowledge, *see* Cooley, 1987 and Nonaka and Takeuchi, 1995). We make it our own by transforming the experience that comes from outside into internal knowledge. Knowledge belongs to us more surely than most of our possessions, and is indeed the most precious and essential of all possessions, because it is what we use to guide our actions in accordance with our values.

Knowledge also depends on memory – and memory too comes in two kinds: internal – inside our heads, and external – knowledge transformed into information (*see* below) and put into external stores like libraries or databases or reference books so that we don't have to try to carry everything we need in our heads.

Information

Information is what human beings transform their knowledge into when they want to communicate it to other people. It is knowledge made visible or audible, in written or printed words, or in speech.[1]

From the point of view of the user, information is what we seek and pay attention to in our outside world when we need to add to or enrich our knowledge in order to act upon it. So we can also usefully think of it as the 'food of knowledge' because

1 'Information allows you to express, transfer and convey knowledge', as Marchand (1997) puts it.

we need information and communication to nourish and maintain our knowledge and keep it in good shape for what we have to do in the world. Without the food of information, knowledge becomes enfeebled.

The transformation of information into knowledge, and knowledge into information, forms the basis for all human learning and communication; it allows ideas to spread across space and time, and links past and present in a network that embraces generations and cultures over millennia. By virtue of that quality, it is also fundamental to the working of organizations of all kinds.

'Two distincts, division none' (Shakespeare, *The Phoenix and the Turtle*)

Knowledge and information are separate but interacting entities; we transform one into another constantly, and according to circumstances one or other will be to the fore. As Samuel Butler is said to have remarked (quoted in Gould, 1991, p268), 'a chicken is merely the egg's way of making another egg'. The critical distinction is that before information can be used it has to be transformed into knowledge in human minds, and then applied by them to affect both the material world and the ideas of others.[2] For these reasons, the policies and strategies discussed in this book need to take into account both information and knowledge, and the term 'information policy' should be understood in that light.

Organizational information policy

An 'organizational information policy' is founded on an organization's overall objectives, and the priorities within them, and defines, at a general level:
● The objectives of information use in the organization, and the priorities among them ● What 'information' means in the context of what the organization is in business for ● The principles on which it will manage information ● Principles for the use of human resources in managing information ● Principles for the use of technology to support information management ● The principles it will apply in relation to establishing the cost-effectiveness of information and knowledge.

An information policy is a dynamic tool which can be used:
● As the basis for developing an organizational information strategy (*see* below)
● To relate everything that is done with information to the organization's overall objectives ● To enable effective decisions on resource allocation ● To promote interaction, communication and mutual support between all parts of the organization, and between the organization and its 'customers' or 'public' ● To provide objective criteria for assessing the results of information-based activities ● To give feedback to the process of developing corporate policies.

Information strategy

Information strategy is the detailed expression of information policy in terms of objectives, targets, and actions to achieve them, for a defined period ahead.

2 Nonaka and Takeuchi (1995, pp58–59) make a similar distinction: 'Knowledge is essentially related to human action.' Information is what 'provides a new point of view for interpreting events or objects, which makes visible previously invisible meanings or sheds light on unexpected connections. ... It affects knowledge by adding something to it or restructuring it.'

Information strategy provides the framework for the management of information. Information strategy, contained within the framework of an organizational policy for information and supported by appropriate systems and technology, is the 'engine' for:

- Maintaining, managing and applying the organization's information resources
- Supporting its essential knowledge base and all who contribute to it, with strategic intelligence, for achieving its key business objectives.

Information management[3]

I give separate definitions of information management and knowledge management here (in line with the 'distinct but interacting' definitions of information and knowledge). The territory which the two domains of information and knowledge management share, and the importance of integrating them, is discussed in Chapter 7 (see pp140–145).

In the context of information policy, information management is the implementation of an information strategy in order to meet information objectives within the overall constraints of available resources. It is therefore concerned with:

- Acquiring, storing, and making accessible information to maintain organizational knowledge, in appropriate information resources • Co-ordinating the information resources that support organizational knowledge and to which people in the organization contribute their knowledge • Providing new resources to meet changes in the environment • Managing information that emerges from knowledge exchanges within the organization and between it and its outside world • Using IS/IT appropriately and innovatively to support knowledge exchanges, interactions, negotiations, and finding, diffusing and communicating information • Making the lessons of experience accessible as an information resource for individual and organizational learning.

Knowledge management

When knowledge management first appeared on the scene, it was in serious danger of being hijacked by the technology to the exclusion of the human activity which is primary – only human minds can know, so the first managers of knowledge have to be the individual owners of the knowing minds. More recently, the balance has been restored, and many writers now give the human element its due (for some examples, see the references and reading list on p11).

In my understanding, knowledge management is concerned with:

- What the people who make up organizations need to know to act successfully in the organization's interests • The actual resources of knowledge and skill belonging to the people who work in an organization, which collectively constitute its knowledge base • Ensuring that these resources are maintained, safeguarded and developed in accordance with the emerging needs of the organization • Supporting individuals in managing the processes of transforming knowledge into infor-

3 The scope of this definition is very close to that of the definition of Information Resource Management, adopted by the Aslib Information Resource Management Network – now the Knowledge and Information Management Network – (see Willard, 1993).

mation and information into knowledge ● Minimizing the costs to individuals and the organization of transforming their knowledge into information and contributing it to the organization's information resources, and maximizing the gains resulting for them ● Helping individuals and the organization to define and keep knowledge rights and obligations ● Promoting knowledge exchanges within the organization and between it and its outside world ● Negotiating limits to what knowledge can and cannot be exchanged ● Systems and technology to support people in using their knowledge ● The value which the use of knowledge contributes to the assets of the organization ● Promoting organizational learning.

(For thoughtful contributions on the concept, *see* Skyrme, 1997 and Wilson, 1998)

Organizations[4]

This definition is designed to be applicable to any kind of organization, from social club to government department; from manufacturing firm to service business; from pressure group to educational institution. Its orientation is towards the humanistic approach typified by 'soft systems' concepts (*see*, for example, Checkland and Holwell, 1998), which places emphasis on the social nature of organizations, and especially on interactions and accommodations among human beings as their essential charactteristic, rather than towards the positivistic, rational decision-making model.

Organizations are:

● Groupings of people for explicit or implicit purposes (even when the purposes are made explicit in 'official' statements, we have to remember that individuals and groups within any organization will have their own interpretations of what they mean) ● Combinations of social and technical systems (organizations can be in trouble if they don't give proper recognition to both kinds of system, if the social and the technical aspects don't match one another, or if the systems aren't appropriate for what the organization aims to do; *see* Eason, 1988).

In meeting their purposes they:

● Create 'offerings' – of products, or services, or combinations of the two – for an 'outside world' of customers, clients, supporters, individuals and organizations which they seek to influence, etc ● Seek 'sustenance' from the outside world to which they direct their offerings, in order to keep in being ● Interact both internally and with their outside world.

---

4 I use the term 'organizations' rather than 'businesses' or 'companies' for what I think are good reasons. Many books are addressed specifically to businesses, telling them how they can use information to compete successfully; that's useful, but not the whole story because:
● The necessity of using information and knowledge strategically isn't confined to the private sector and businesses that sell goods/services
● Society and the economy don't depend exclusively on such businesses
● Businesses need government and other public organizations which use knowledge and information effectively
● Society, at all levels and in all its transactions and interactions, can be fouled up if public as well as private organizations don't use knowledge and information well
● And it's not just businesses that need to compete, nor is competition the antithesis of colπlaboration. Both businesses and public organizations need both, and to do both successfully and to know when to compete and when to collaborate, they all need to use knowledge and information strategically.

Process

The process view of organizations, as defined, for example, by Best (1996, p4) – 'For practical purposes we may regard a process ... as the set of resources and activities (whether undertaken by people or by machines) necessary and sufficient to convert some input into some output' – sees them as an interlocking series of activities devoted to creating outputs, instead of a set of functional departments within the bounds of which self-contained activities take place – the metaphor is a river, rather than a stack of boxes.

This book takes a process approach in two ways. First it looks at the business of developing information policy and strategy as an overall process, containing a series of processes and sub-processes, in all of which human minds, assisted as necessary by technology, use knowledge to convert what exists into something new. Second, it follows Davenport (1993) in seeing information as something that enters into all business processes, and that is essential for integrating all the processes that make up an organization.

References

BAWDEN, D. (2001), 'The shifting terminologies of information', *Aslib Proceedings*, 53 (3) 93–98.

BEST, D. (ed) (1996), *The Fourth Resource: Information and its Management*, Aldershot: Aslib/Gower.

CHECKLAND, P. and HOLWELL, S. (1998), *Information, Systems and Information Systems. Making sense of the field*, Chichester: John Wiley and Sons.

COOLEY, M. (1987), *Architect or Bee? The human price of technology*, London: Hogarth Press.

DAVENPORT, T. H. (1993), *Process innovation. Reengineering work through information technology*, Boston, MA: Harvard Business School Press.

EASON, K. (1988), *Information technology and organisational change*, London: Taylor and Francis.

GOULD, S. J. (1991), *Ever since Darwin*, London: Penguin Books.

MARCHAND, D. (1997), 'Competing with information: Know what you want'. *FT Mastering Management Reader*, July/August 1997.

NONAKA, I. and TAKEUCHI, H. (1995). *The Knowledge-creating company: how Japanese companies create the dynamics of information*, New York: Oxford University Press.

SKYRME, D. J. (1997), 'Knowledge management: oxymoron or dynamic duo?', *Managing Information*, 4 (7), 24–26.

WILSON, O. (1998), 'Knowledge management: putting a good idea to work', *Managing Information*, 5 (2), 31–33.

WILLARD, N. (1993), 'Information resources management', *Aslib Information*, 21 (5) 201–205.

Other useful reading

BONFIELD, P. (1999), Knowledge Management Strategy at BT, *Managing Information* 6 (6) 21–29. 'computers do not "know" as humans know'. And we need to focus on culture, strategy and performance first. 'Then when we are sure about the ends we are seeking, we can let the techies loose on the means.'

STREATFIELD, D. and WILSON, T. (1999), 'Deconstructing "knowledge management"' *Aslib Proceedings*, 51 (3) 67–71. 'We cannot manage knowledge directly – we can only manage information about the knowledge possessed by people in organisations.'

WILLARD, N. (1999), 'Knowledge Management, foundations for a secure structure', *Managing Information*, 6 (5) 45–49. 'Knowledge Management is the development and facilitation of collaborative working, recognising the interconnected nature of people, processes and information ...'

Introduction

About this book

How it came to be written and why

The story of this book goes back many years – to a consultancy assignment in an organization which wanted to set up an information service and appoint a professional manager to run it. My job was to analyse their information needs, define what the new service should do to meet them, and advise on the appointment of the manager. When the main work was done and the manager had taken up the post, a few days of consultancy time remained for us to do some joint planning. Reckoning that, although the organization had taken a commendable initiative about information, it was entering new territory of which it knew comparatively little, we decided to use the time in working out what we called an organizational information policy and getting top management to sign up to it. We both knew from experience that organizations are liable to take initiatives and then, as time goes by and other concerns become important, or new fashions take their fancy, fail to go on supporting them. We wanted to protect this one from such a fate, and to ensure that the service and its manager received continuing understanding and support from above, and guaranteed resources to develop the work that had been agreed on.

The policy that we produced was based on working out the information implications of the organization's main objectives; that analysis led to a short statement of an information policy which committed it to:

1 Draw on all appropriate resources of information, originating outside the organization, or from its own activities, to meet the needs of the organization and its staff in fulfilling their objectives

2 Organize the resources of information in appropriate systems, using suitable means of information handling

3 Promote inter-relations between the various information-handling systems, and to develop interaction and feedback between users and providers of information, so that the development of the organization's information activities is fully integrated with its policies.

The information manager put the policy to active use, and it fulfilled its purpose for several years, during which the service developed, expanded its remit, acquired more resources, initiated work towards an information strategy and took part in joint development of an IT strategy. Our conclusion, looking back nearly ten years later, was that 'an agreed information policy has been "politically" useful as a basis for taking initiatives and making cases for resources for development, and as a tool for raising the awareness of management about the values of information.' (Orna, 1990). Not long after that, changes in the organization's orientation and personnel led to stagnation and decline in the role of the service. In the last year or so, however, things have begun to progress again; the significance of information strategy has been rediscovered under the stimulus of the popularity of knowledge management – and it has been possible to take advantage of it by returning to the foundation created by the original information policy, and relating it to the organization's current orientation and goals.

My impression that there weren't many organizational information policies about was confirmed at a conference of senior information professionals in 1988, when a speaker asked how many of the delegates came from organizations that had a specific information policy. Only four hands out of over 100 were raised. So I submitted a proposal to a publisher, which led to what I think was the first book devoted to the idea that organizations need policies for information just as they do for marketing, or R&D. That was published in 1990. When the time came for a new edition eight years later, there had been so many changes in the information world, that I wrote what was essentially a new book (Orna, 1999) to take account of them, though it was still based on the fundamental ideas that had inspired the first.

My greatest satisfaction from writing the first and second editions of the book has come from meeting people who have told me it had helped them clarify their ideas, make sense of their experience, and take useful action in their own environment: information managers who had used it to prepare for an interview and to get a job they wanted, or to carry through an information audit or make a successful business case for an information policy; and senior managers of global businesses who were able to draw on it in formulating information strategy.

At the same time, students and their teachers in institutions I visited to give lectures, and staff in businesses where I was carrying out consultancy assignments, made me aware that there were people who were likely to be involved in the processes which formed the core of the book, who needed a short practical text. They wanted:
• A reliable account of the key processes, with realistic ideas on carrying it through, drawn from actual practice • A sound framework of the ideas underlying the practice recommended, into which they could build their own experience and their special knowledge, and which they could relate to their own context • Advice and ideas from experience about how to deal with problems likely to be encountered on the way, and get the best from being involved in the process.

I am very glad that now there is an opportunity to provide what they seek.

The readers to whom this book is addressed

This book is particularly addressed to:
1 Those preparing to enter all areas of the information profession, particularly those oriented towards managing information resources and information content (in jobs with both traditional and contemporary titles – information service managers, librarians, information systems managers, records managers, knowledge managers, information resource managers, content managers, etc); but also those specializing in the systems and IT that create the infrastructure which supports all those activities
2 Working professionals of other kinds, whose job requires them to acquire, use, communicate and exchange information and knowledge, and who may have an information-management element as part if it (eg being responsible for a database, managing records for a specific activity, recording and updating procedures, etc)

3 Managers without a specific information background, who are either the line managers of people who are professionally or incidentally engaged in managing information; or who are charged with overseeing projects such as information audits, or the development of knowledge or information strategies.

It is emphatically not addressed to what the staff of one organization of my acquaintance calls, more or less affectionately, 'TOTO' (The Top of The Organization). I find books which set out to tell 'business leaders' how to succeed in using information either unconvincing or difficult to read or both. Some offer them rules, recipes, and 'tool kits', 'instrument panels' or other bits of ironmongery; others present useful ideas, but wrapped up in academic jargon which suggests that they are really addressed to fellow academics in the management schools. Neither of those is my scene, but should any TOTO readers find their way here, they are truly welcome, and they may well find something useful in it.

The content

The central part of this book (Chapters 2–6) consists of chapters from the second edition of my book *Practical Information Policies*, Edition 2 (Orna, 1999) which describe the essential process of developing information policy and strategy for organizations. A good deal has happened in the information world since I wrote them, and I have extended my ideas and learned from experience in that time too; so each of these chapters has a postscript, under the heading of 'Practical Insights', which embodies some of that new thinking and learning.

Many organizations and businesses today engage in the processes described in those chapters. They do so because they believe some or all of these propositions:
• Information and knowledge are assets that have accountable value • Used strategically (ie in line with an overall business strategy) they can bring: success in competing; leadership in whatever their markets are and recognition as leaders in 'best practice'; success in doing whatever they're in business to do and/or survival in turbulent weather • An 'information and/or knowledge architecture' (a combination of IT/systems infrastructure and ways of managing information content) is necessary for success, and because they believe information auditing and strategy development based on it are necessary steps on the way to achieving the value they seek.

The trouble with beliefs of this kind at the top is that they can be transient and without secure foundations of understanding. That's bad luck for those who are made responsible for carrying out the processes based on them for their organizations. So they need to be armed with clear ideas, good arguments, and practical ways of setting about it that can win conviction, and earn assent and resources for getting on with doing the job and implementing the results. I have tried to provide this for every stage in the book, and particularly in two entirely new final chapters.

Chapter 7 recapitulates the main themes, with particular emphasis on important new thinking about them and the lessons for information strategy, so that readers can make them their own, illuminate them with their own experience and knowledge, and use them in practice, on the way towards developing and using information strategy. The eighth and last chapter looks at specific situations that readers may encounter – particularly as they move towards transforming findings into recommendations and recommendations into action – and suggests ways of dealing with them based on practical experience.

Organizations and information

To make a bridge between this introduction and the chapters which follow, let us now consider the essentials about organizations, which form the context in which most of us spend our working lives, and why they need information and human knowledge to survive and prosper.

What makes an organization?

We all know what organizations are; we work for them, we use their services, pay our taxes to them, belong to them to pursue our hobbies or hobby-horses (though, according to the *Shorter Oxford Dictionary,* the use of the word to mean 'an organized body, system or society' dates back only to 1873). The definition suggested earlier to cover all kinds of organizations (*see* p10) can be summarized as:
• A grouping of human beings • For explicit or implicit purpose • Creating 'offerings' of products and/or services • Interacting, internally, and with its 'outside world' • Seeking sustenance to keep itself in being • Having a structure and a boundary • Embodying both social and technical systems.

What do organizations need to know to survive?

If those are the distinguishing characteristics of organizations, then in order to keep alive and well there are certain things that *every* organization needs to know:
• What is happening inside its boundaries • What is happening in its 'outside world' of customers, members, clients, competitors, suppliers, markets, providers of grants-in-aid, supporters, donors, institutions and individuals it needs to influence • How to create appropriate 'offerings' for its outside world • How to communicate, within itself, and with its outside world.

Why do they need to define for themselves what constitutes knowledge and information?

I have given working definitions of knowledge and information at the beginning of this book (*see* pp7–8). Why am I now saying that each organization has to make its own definition of what constitutes knowledge and information for it?

Reason, and experience, show that it is necessary. If we look at the list I have just given of the things that each organization needs to know, it's evident that the actual content of each element of knowledge and know-how, and of the information needed to maintain them in good health, will be highly specific, and dependent on how individual organizations define what they are in business for. What is vital information for one can be quite irrelevant for another.

The next chapter sets out in some detail how to arrive at a definition of:
• 'The knowledge and information this organization needs in order to achieve its goals' • How the organization needs to use knowledge and information • How they need to flow inside the organization and between it and its outside world. Here, it may be helpful to quote examples of two organizations (*see also* Orna, 1999, pp233–249 and 325–342), to show just how different are the kinds of information which they need to take in to maintain their knowledge (*see* Table 1.1, over).

Credit Union Services Corporation Australia	Surrey Police UK
Credit Unions, in Australia and world-wide	Trends in crime – local, national, international
Developments in the economy, finance, industry, socio-demographic trends	Local population: age profile, employment
Legal and regulatory compliance requirements	All legislation relevant to policework
Customer response to products	Relevant IT developments; eg imaging; hand-held devices for remote access to in-house databases
Competitors – banks and building societies	Research in criminology
Existing and potential markets	Local geography, land use, vehicle movements
Contacts, and the organizations it needs to communicate with and influence	Local organizations/institutions Contacts: individual, and in local and national organizations
	Other police forces in the UK and abroad

Table 1.1
Essential information from the outside world as defined for two organizations

Why organizations need a policy and a strategy for information
(for definitions, *see* pp8–9)

If the knowledge that organizations need, and the information resources they require to keep it in good health, are so wide-ranging, and so specific and individual in content, then managing them must be based on a clear, accepted organizational policy. The effort invested in developing a policy and then a strategy for using knowledge and information, *and in applying them,* can bring both avoidance of dangers and positive benefits.

Keeping out of danger

Table 1.2 (*see* opposite) summarizes some of the dangers identified from events in real organizations, that could be minimized or avoided entirely by applying appropriate policies and strategies for using information.

Benefits to gain

Mere possession of something called an organizational information policy is, of course, no guarantee of avoiding risks or gaining benefits. A policy acquires value only when thinking human beings get together to put it to use. When that happens, it becomes a framework of reference, securely attached to the organization's business strategy, within which it can build strategies, standards, procedures, rules for how people use information and knowledge. As such it can promote productive links

Situation	Consequent risks and losses
The organization hasn't defined • What it needs to know • The information it needs • How people need to use knowledge and information	Failure to: Meet customers' needs; realize opportunities; compete successfully; meet legal requirements
Senior management doesn't understand the need for professional management of information and knowledge, or what information professionals do	Insecure resources for information services, erratic cuts, lack of information and continuity; professional information skills not properly used
People have to undertake information responsibilities without adequate support and training	Information resources inadequately managed, without co-ordination; can't be fully used
Unco-ordinated information activities, resources, and systems	Incomplete exploitation of information; anarchic use; failures to find everything relevant in seeking information
Inappropriate information activities; information presented in unhelpful formats for the intended users	Time wasted on doing things that don't need doing at all, or that could be done more effectively; people's time wasted disentangling information they need
Poor communication of essential information for creating the organization's products and services	Failures in attempts to innovate; customers/clients don't get what they require; loss of market share to competition
Systems and IT investment without strategy related to overall business objectives	IS/IT infrastructure fails to make maximum contribution to the organization's core competencies; and to give maximum support to information users
New knowledge gained by staff not transformed into information and not made accessible in the organization's information resources	Loss of potential value; failure to communicate; lost opportunities to create new knowledge and innovate
Outcomes of actions not adequately recorded; failures and mistakes buried	No learning; repetition of things that don't work; risk of bad publicity from repeated errors
Management don't fully understand what they need to know to anticipate dangers, how to get the information they need, how to make good use of it	Inability to anticipate and respond appropriately to internal or external threat
Organization doesn't understand the importance of accurate and ethical use of information in dealing with its outside world	Loss of reputation, of customers, of money in compensating and rectifying, of support

Table 1.2
Risks and losses that information policy can
help to avoid

Changes promoted by policy	Resulting benefits
Integrated information activities	All resources of information can contribute to all organization's objectives
Information policy integrated within corporate policies and priorities	Decisions about resources for information activities taken in relation to how they contribute to corporate goals
Established criteria for assessing how information contributes to achieving organizational objectives	Off-the-cuff decisions to cut information resources become less likely, because effects can be predicted
Distributed knowledge of all information resources and activities is brought together	Promotes co-operation, negotiation and openness among people responsible for different aspects of information management
Information flows more freely	Innovation, productivity and competitiveness are better supported
Options for investment in systems and IT can be evaluated in relation to key organizational goals, and to what people need to do with information to achieve them	Basis for sound systems and IT strategy, supporting corporate goals, and allowing productive use of technology
Intelligence gathering and constant monitoring of internal and external environment supported as part of information policy	Not only timely response to change, but chance to initiate change by taking advantage of changing environments
Exchanges of knowledge and information encouraged and supported; technology helps staff to transform new knowledge to accessible information and add it to information resources	'Knowledge sharing' becomes a reality rather than a slogan; new knowledge can be used to add value to organization's offerings

Table 1.3
Benefits which an organizational information policy can help to promote

with the organization's other strategies (IS/IT, human resources, marketing, customer relations, competition, for example); allow job descriptions that define what the holders need to do with information, and the people with whom they need to exchange knowledge and information; provide for transfer of knowledge when people leave the organization. Table 1.3 summarizes the main potential benefits.

That marks the end of the beginning; I have tried in this chapter to tell readers enough to allow them to get something useful from the rest of the book. Now we can move on to look at the processes that lead to productive organizational information policies and strategies.

References
DRUCKER, P. (1995), *Managing in a Time of Great Change*, Oxford: Butterworth Heinemann.
ORNA, E. (1990), *Practical Information Policies, how to manage information flow in organizations*, Aldershot: Gower.
ORNA, E. (1999), *Practical Information Policies* (Ed2), Aldershot: Gower.

*All healthy organizations generate and use knowledge. As organizations interact
with their environments, they absorb information, turn it into knowledge, and
take action based on it in combination with their experiences, values, and internal
rules. They sense and respond. Without knowledge, an organization could not
organize itself, it would be unable to maintain itself as a functioning enterprise.*
–DAVENPORT, T. and PRUSAK, L. (1998), p52

A basis of understanding, and why we need it

Whatever we aim to do about the way an organization uses information, and wherever the initiative comes from, before we take any decisions we need as clear an
understanding as we can get of the organization: what it seeks to achieve, where it
is trying to go, how it sets about its business, and how it sees itself and its outside
world. That is the only safe basis for action designed to lead to change in how it
uses information and applies knowledge.

The positive gains from starting in this way are:
● A picture of 'what should be' – if this is what the organization is trying to do,
with this structure and this culture, then this is what it ought to be trying to do
with information and knowledge ● Some first ideas about how that could be
expressed in a policy for information, and a first definition of what information
means for the organization ● Practical leads for the next steps in the process,
for example an information audit, or development of an information strategy:
○ Where to concentrate effort ○ Where to start ○ Key people to involve; potential
management supporters, allies to cultivate, foes to neutralize ○ The right questions to ask ○ Benefits to look for ○ Appropriate ways of setting about the job.

Initiatives for starting

The opportunity for starting this process may come in a number of ways. The initiative may come from management, or it may originate from senior professional
staff who are particularly concerned with information. It may arise out of a range of
situations: a clearly formulated intention to move towards a corporate strategy for
information; management's fancy being taken by a new topic such as 'knowledge
management', or a fashionable technique like information auditing; a response to a
particular question – such as how to give a geographically dispersed and professional staff direct access from their desktop to essential business information; or
even a negative and threatening situation, where enterprising people use crisis as
'the coin of opportunity'.

If the initiative comes from the top, these days it is quite likely to be for the
development of a strategy – either for information or for information systems/IT,
thanks to the IMPACT programme and the Hawley Committee (1995) and to similar
developments specifically addressed to board level, which have helped to create

more information awareness at the top of enlightened organizations. Many initiatives, however, will still be in response to a particular situation with an information aspect, often defined in terms that are far from expressing the real problem. It is one of the aims of this book to encourage decision-makers to use specific situations as an opportunity for starting an investigation which will lead to a picture of what the organization as a whole should be doing with information, and to the beginnings of a policy, and which will, by virtue of that, have a much better chance of yielding a productive solution to the original problem.

Another aim is to encourage experienced information professionals who hold a position of authority in the management structure, and have won respect for their judgement by their achievements, to take initiatives of this kind, and to see it as part of their role to educate management and their colleagues in the gains to be made through strategic management of the organization's resources of information and knowledge. At the start of the 1990s (Orna, 1990) I noted the loss of self-esteem that the information profession seemed to be suffering; there is still quite a lot of that about, and still evidence of great ignorance of the significance of information and the capabilities of information professionals among the managers of many organizations. Abell (1996), for example, reports that, while many companies are becoming more interested in information utilization, real innovation and developments are being driven by people other than information professionals, and that the latter are not seen as being part of the business. On the other hand, recent experience (*see* for instance the case studies in Orna, 1999), suggests some positive changes. I have certainly encountered more information professionals exercising high levels of authority, who are taking and making opportunities to move their organizations towards information strategy, often in new alliances with colleagues from different professional backgrounds.

Extracting meaning from objectives

We have to start here before we can begin to think about what the organization does with information, because its objectives and priorities – its own definition of what it exists for – make the framework within which everything we learn about it will be interpreted, all possible courses of action evaluated, and all decisions implemented. And if we don't fully understand what it thinks it is in business for, we risk misinterpreting what we find at later stages, assigning inappropriate values to information resources, and choosing information solutions that are so bad a match that they harm its interests rather than furthering them. An associated problem is the well-attested fact that even when organizations have detailed statements of their objectives (and that is not universal), it can't be taken for granted either that everyone knows about them, or that there is general agreement on what they mean. None the less, objectives make a starting point, and the very fact of making and presenting a reasoned analysis of their knowledge and information implications can provide a focus for productive discussion of their meaning.

Table 2.1 presents a 'worked example' based on the objectives of one of the case study organizations in Orna (1999). We start from the top-level set of objectives, and we ask of each of them: 'To achieve this objective, what knowledge and/or know-how do we require?'

Objectives	Knowledge requirements
To:	About:
• Maintain and improve the performance of companies and the securities and futures markets	The companies and markets covered by its remit The economic and financial context in which they operate, home and worldwide Government policies in relation to them The work of comparable institutions in other countries
• Maintain investor confidence in the securities and futures markets by ensuring adequate investor protection	Investors, institutional and individual, and their investments Risks against which investor protection is needed
• Achieve uniformity in the way it performs its functions and exercises its powers	How it defines its functions and powers and how it carries out the functions and uses the powers
• Administer laws effectively, with a minimum of procedural requirements	The laws which it has to administer The methods and procedures it uses in doing so
• Process and store documents and information which people give the Commission efficiently and quickly • Ensure that they are available to the public as soon as possible	The documents and information it collects from its 'outside world' How it manages their processing and storage How it makes them available to the public How well it meets their requirements
• Take whatever action is necessary to enforce the law	How it identifies when action is needed, decides on what to do, takes action The results

Table 2.1
The objectives of an organization (The Australian Securities and Investments Commission) and what it needs to know to achieve them[1]

The set of answers to that question provides the basis for the next question: 'What information do we need to draw on to maintain the knowledge we require?' As will be seen from Table 2.2 (*see* pp22–24), the answers become more complex and detailed when we get to this level, and more meaning starts to emerge from the original objectives.

We now have to think about what the Commission's staff have to do with the information it needs in order to achieve its objectives. Here things become yet more complex, because we have to consider not only who needs to use the information, but also the information flows and interactions that are required both within the Commission and between it and its outside world. Table 2.3 (*see* pp27–32) starts

1 The Commission's overall aim is 'to protect the interests of companies and investors ... ensure fair play in business, prevent corporate crime, protect investors and help Australia's business reputation abroad.'

Knowledge requirements	Information required to maintain knowledge	
About	Content	'Containers'
• The companies and markets covered by its remit	Ownership Structure Performance data	Relevant external databases Internal databases Specialist press Statistical series
	Products and services	Company information products
• The economic and financial context in which they operate, home and world-wide	National and worldwide economic situation Market conditions	Relevant external databases Internet Specialist press Statistical series
• Government policies in relation to them	Legislation Planned developments	Government publications Government websites Parliamentary debates Reports of government bodies Contacts in federal and state governments
• The work of comparable institutions in other countries	Location, constitution, methods	Annual reports Contacts, correspondence
• Investors, institutional and individual, and their investments	Who they are Their investments Their experience and views of companies and markets	Specialist press Reports on research by Commission and others Reports from staff in contact with investors
• Risks against which investor protection is needed	Ways in which investors have suffered loss Opinion of protection afforded	Specialist press Internal database Records of complaints Reports on research by Commission and others
• How it defines its functions and powers and how it carries out the functions and uses the powers	Current definition and proposed changes in scope	Legislation establishing the Commission Reports of government bodies
• The laws which it has to administer	Existing law and proposed changes	Relevant legislation Reports of government bodies

Table 2.2
The information (content and 'containers')
which the Commission needs to draw on to
maintain its knowledge

continued on next page

Knowledge requirements	Information required to maintain knowledge	
About:	Content	'Containers'
• The methods and procedures it uses	Methods and procedures established by the Commission	Manuals, minutes, guidance instructions
	Performance criteria and results	Standards and criteria statements; reports on performance in meeting them
	People responsible for these activities; qualifications, skills, training	Personnel and training records held in database
	IT and systems used to support them	Reports on IT/IS management Specialist press for keeping track of relevant development
• The documents and information it collects from its 'outside world'	What companies tell investors about their products/services, activities, results	Prospectuses, company reports, takeover documents, etc
	Records of Comission's dealings with companies	Internal database of companies and Commission's transactions with them
• How it manages their processing and storage	Information management strategy	Strategic Information Plan
• How it makes them available to the public	Information systems strategy	Corporate IT Strategy Plan
• How well it meets their requirements	Questions put by inquirers	Records of transactions with inquirers via electronic inquiry service; reports
	Their views of service offered	Reports of user surveys; information audits, etc
	Performance criteria and results	Standards and criteria statements; reports on performance in meeting them
	People responsible for these activities; qualifications, skills, training	Personnel and training records held in database
	IT and systems used to support them	Reports on IT/IS management Specialist press for keeping track of relevant developments

Table 2.2

continued on next page

Knowledge requirements	Information required to maintain knowledge	
About:	Content	'Containers'
• How it identifies when action is needed, decides on what to do, takes action	The Commission's transactions with investors and companies	Correspondence; records of transactions; visit reports; reports of investigations
	Decisions and rationales for them	Internal reports Communications with Director of Public Prosecutions
• The outcomes of action	Results and lessons from them	Internal reports; database; Annual Report
	Performance criteria and results	Standards and criteria statements; reports on performance in meeting them
	People responsible for these activities; qualifications, skills, training	Personnel and training records held in database
	IT and systems used to support them	Reports on IT/IS management Specialist press for keeping track of relevant development

Table 2.2 *end*

from the kinds of information the Commission has been identified as requiring, and sets out for each how it needs to flow, and the people who need to interact with one another in order to transform it into knowledge and act on it.

So far as I know, this is an exercise seldom if ever undertaken in organizations, though it seems quite an obvious step. Experience shows that people concerned with information management have no difficulty with the concept, or with deriving knowledge and information needs from the objectives of their own organization. And it usually takes no more than a few hours to produce the answers.

Given that in any organization there will almost certainly be different interpretations of objectives, and different degrees of knowledge of them, a straightforward analysis of this kind makes a good starting point for discussion of what they mean, and of what information means for the organization. Using something like this as a starter helps people who are not much in the habit of thinking about such topics to grasp them and relate them to their own work.

'What should be'

Let us now develop from this analysis a brief statement of its implications for what the Commission should be doing with information in order to maintain the knowledge it needs in good health and ready for effective action.

What the Commission needs to know

The most important knowledge for the Commission is that about:
• Companies • Markets • The economic and social context • Relevant government policies • Investors and their investments • Risks against which investors should be protected • Its own functions and powers and how it exercises them • The laws it has to administer, and how it does so • The information it collects from its 'outside world' • How it manages that information • How well it meets the requirements of the public • How it takes action, and the results.

The information resources it needs to feed its knowledge

To maintain its knowledge, the Commission needs to acquire and have ready access to:
• Information about the companies and markets covered by its remit, in internal and external databases, textual and numeric forms • Qualitative and quantitative reports generated from its own activities • Externally originating reference and information products relevant to its 'outside world', in various media, print-on-paper and electronic • 'Intelligence' products, resulting from in-house work, and bought in • Information about its own resources of knowledge and expertise • Information about its own performance and the criteria by which it is judged • Archives and records

The human resources the Commission needs to manage the information resources

The Commission needs people who can manage acquisition and maintenance, and provide access to the various resources of information, who can gather strategic intelligence and interpret it, who can integrate and add value to the whole range of information resources, and who understand existing information needs and are able to anticipate emerging ones in the light of the company's key business objectives. It also needs to assign responsibility for awareness of the totality of information resources and information activities, and for promoting their integrated use.

And, besides those with special responsibility for managing information, everyone who uses it needs to understand their own obligations and what they owe to their colleagues in that respect.

The information interactions the Commission needs

The value of information to organizations is realized only when human minds transform it into knowledge, combine it with what they already know, and, supported by appropriate information technology, act on it in co-operation – the process which Skyrme (1992) describes as 'knowledge networking'. So information flows, interactions and negotiations between people are the most critical part of 'what should be'. The analysis of Table 2.3 could be taken into yet more detail, but even at the present level, it is obvious that the Commission needs to provide organizational structures and cultural encouragement for many interactions, both internally and between itself and the outside world. To take only the interactions necessary to achieve the first objective concerning the performance of companies and the securities and futures markets (*see* p21): they require the participation of company staff, industry associations, local business communities, programme managers and staff responsible for contact with companies, Intelligence and Analysis Service, records managers, information professionals, systems/IT staff, and those responsible for publicity.

The systems and IT infrastructure the company needs

If we follow through all the information interactions required for achieving the Commission's goals, it quickly becomes obvious that in almost all of them the contribution of systems and IT is essential to support people in reaching the information they need, and in using it for their own purposes. It is important to observe the 'chronology' of this contribution. Systems and IT cannot make their input effectively until the organization has defined the information it needs to support people in using their knowledge; that has to be the basis of the brief for creating the technical infrastructure and the applications that do the right job. This seems so obvious that it is almost embarrassing to mention it – but not quite; there are too many examples of management failing in its obligations to create the brief, and leaving systems and IT to do the best they can, often with less than happy results. Sillince (1994), for example, shows how implementation of a systems change in production management in manufacturing companies (the introduction of hybrid MRP2/JIT – Materials Requirements Planning/Just In Time – systems) is undermined by lack of attention to information needs and use, combined with structural and cultural factors.

On the other hand, Abell (1996) reports that organizations are becoming less dependent on IT departments to develop information strategies, and more interested in an information systems or information utilization focus. Certainly over the past few years I have come across organizations which have started by trying to develop an 'information systems strategy' and which have realized in due course (often prompted by systems staff) that what they really need is a strategy for information. In this connection, Symon et al (1992) provide some interesting insights; they describe an action research approach to a project to develop a hospital information system which took into account information interactions, organizational structure and organizational culture, and led to a framework of information needs and an implementation strategy.

What organizational structure and culture can tell us

Analysis starting from what the organization says it is trying to do can, as we have just seen, take us a long way, but it's not to be relied on by itself. We need to look at it in the light of the organization's history, structure and culture, because that will cast into relief the strengths we can build on, the threats we shall have to avoid, the impregnable bastions which will withstand direct attack, and the strategic alliances to be sought.

Many researchers have described features of organizations which seem to favour productive and profitable use of information. A programme to study the relation-
continued on p32

Information strategy in practice

Companies and markets covered by its remit

People involved

- Company staff responsible for supplying information to the Commission
- Industry associations
- Local business communities

- Programme managers and staff responsible for contact with companies
- Intelligence and Analysis Service
- Staff responsible for company records
- Librarians and other information specialists
- Systems/IT staff [1]
- Staff responsible for publicizing the Commission's work

Interactions/information flow

between	• Company staff responsible for supplying information to the Commission • Industry associations • Local business communities	*and*	• Programme managers and staff responsible for contact with companies
between	• Staff responsible and for contact with companies	*and*	• Intelligence and Analysis Service • Staff responsible for company records • Librarians and other information specialists • Systems/IT staff • Staff responsible for providing information about the Commission's work

1 Systems/IT staff are concerned in nearly all information interactions, because they are responsible for ensuring that systems and IT support people in using information in the ways that they need

The economic and financial context in which they operate, home and worldwide

People involved

- Suppliers

- Intelligence and Analysis Service
- Librarians and other information specialists
- Decision makers about strategy; those responsible for implementing it
- Systems/IT staff

Interactions/information flow

between	• Intelligence and Analysis Service • Librarians and other information specialists	*and*	• Suppliers • Decision makers about strategy; those responsible for implementing it • Systems/IT staff

---

Table 2.3

continued on the next page

The information flows and interactions among All information flows are in both directions effective use of the knowledge and information the Commission requires

Note:
All information flows are in both directions

People involved

- Government; public service
- MPs

- Decision makers and staff responsible for government contacts
- Intelligence and Analysis Service
- Librarians and other information specialists
- Systems/IT staff

Interactions/information flow

between	• Government; public service • MPs	*and*	• Decision makers and staff respons-ible for Government contacts
between	• Decision makers and staff respons-ible for government contacts	*and*	• Intelligence and Analysis Service • Librarians and other information specialists • Systems/IT staff

The work of comparable institutions in other countries

People involved

- Staff of comparable institutions

- External relations staff
- Programme managers
- Librarians and other information specialists

Interactions/information flow

between	• Staff of comparable institutions	*and*	• External relations staff
between	• External relations staff	*and*	• Programme managers • Librarians and other information specialists

Investors, institutional and individual, and their investments

People involved

- Investors

- Staff responsible for investor contacts
- Staff responsible for publicizing the Commission's work
- Intelligence and Analysis Service
- Librarians and other information specialists
- Systems/IT staff

Table 2.3   *continued on next page*

Investors, institutional and individual, and their investments *(continued)*

Interactions/information flow

between	• Investors	*and*	• Staff responsible for investor contacts • Staff responsible for providing information about the Commission's work
between	• Staff responsible for investor contacts • Staff responsible for providing information about the Commission's work	*and*	• Intelligence and Analysis Services • Librarians and other information specialists • Systems/IT staff

Risks against which investor protection is needed

People involved

- Investors
- Companies

- Staff responsible for investor and company contacts
- Intelligence and Analysis Service
- Librarians and other information specialists
- Staff responsible for publicizing the Commission's work

Interactions/information flow

between	• Investors • Companies	*and*	• Staff responsible for investor and company contacts
between	• Staff responsible for investor and company contacts	*and*	• Intelligence and Analysis Services • Librarians and other information specialists • Staff responsible for providing information about the Commission's work

How it carries out its functions and uses its powers

People involved

- All staff of the Commission
- Staff responsible for monitoring performance
- Systems/IT staff

Interactions/information flow

between	• Staff responsible for monitoring performance	*and*	• All staff of the Commission • Systems/IT staff

Table 2.3

continued on next page

The laws which it has to administer

People involved

- Legislators
- Professional legal staff
- Staff responsible for contacts with companies and investors

Interactions/information flow

between	• Legislators	*and*	• Professional legal staff
between	• Professional legal staff	*and*	• Staff responsible for contacts with companies and investors

The methods and procedures it uses in doing so

People involved

- All staff of the Commission
- Staff responsible for developing and maintaining methods and procedures
- Staff responsible for monitoring performance

Interactions/information flow

between	• Staff responsible for developing and recording and maintaining methods and procedures • Staff responsible for monitoring performance	*and*	• All staff of the Commission

The documents and information it collects from its 'outside world'. How it manages their processing and storage. How it makes them available to the public

People involved

- Providers of documents and information
- Members of the public who make inquiries

- Staff responsible for collecting documents and information
- Staff responsible for processing and storing them
- Staff responsible for making them accessible
- Staff who need access to them
- Staff who deal with inquiries from outside
- Systems/IT staff

Interactions/information flow

between	• Providers of documents and information	*and*	• Staff responsible for collecting documents and information

Table 2.3 *continued on next page*

The documents and information it collects from its 'outside world'. How it manages their processing and storage. How it makes them available to the public *(continued)*

Interactions/information flow

between	• Staff responsible for collecting documents and information	*and*	• Staff responsible for processing and storing them • Staff responsible for making them accessible
between	• Staff responsible for processing and storing them	*and*	• Staff who need access to them • Staff who deal with inquiries from outside
between	• Staff responsible for making them accessible	*and*	• Systems/IT staff
between	• Members of the public who make inquiries	*and*	• Staff who deal with inquiries

How well it meets the requirements of inquirers

People involved

- Members of the public who make inquiries
- Staff who deal with inquiries
- Staff responsible for managing documents and information
- Staff responsible for monitoring performance
- Systems/IT staff

Interactions/information flow

between	• Members of the public who make inquiries	*and*	• Staff who deal with inquiries
between	• Staff who deal with inquiries	*and*	• Staff responsible for managing documents and information • Systems/IT staff
between	• Staff who deal with inquiries • Staff responsible for managing documents and information	*and*	• Staff responsible for monitoring performance • Systems/IT staff

How it identifies when action is needed, decides on what to do, takes action

People involved

- Companies
- Investors
- Director of Public Prosecutions
- Civil courts
- Staff responsible for contact with companies
- Staff responsible for investor contacts

Table 2.3

continued on next page

People involved (continued)

- Staff responsible for initiating action
- Intelligence and Analysis Service
- Staff responsible for company records
- Systems/IT staff

Interactions/information flow

between
- Staff responsible for contact with companies
- Staff responsible for investor contacts

and
- Staff responsible for initiating action
- Intelligence and Analysis Service
- Staff responsible for company records
- Systems/IT staff

between
- Staff responsible for initiating action *and*
- Direct of Public Prosecutions
- Civil courts

The results

People involved

between
- Staff responsible for initiating action
- Staff responsible for contact with companies
- Staff responsible for investor contacts
- Staff responsible for company records
- Staff responsible for publicizing the Commission's work

Interactions/information flow

between
- Staff responsible for initiating action

and
- Staff responsible for contact with companies
- Staff responsible for investor contacts
- Staff responsible for company records
- Staff responsible for publicizing the Commission's work
- Staff who deal with inquiries

Table 2.3 *end*

ship between information culture and business performance in Finland (Ginman, 1987) observed linkages between the factors of the CEO's information culture, company culture, the 'life cycle' stage the company was at, and its business performance (*see* Figure 2.1). Ginman concludes that there seems to be 'a strong connection between intellectual and material resource transformation' and that 'the supply of information to companies must be designed to comply with their prevailing culture and requirements.' (p105). Her observations, particularly about the importance of the CEO in promoting an information ethos, are confirmed in follow-up work by Owens and Wilson (1996) (*see also* Abell and Winterman, 1993 for a literature review on information culture and business performance).

Skyrme (1992), writing from experience of Digital Equipment Corporation's attempts to develop knowledge networking, describes the organizational factors that go with success as:

> ● A degree of informality ● Knowledge authority rather than position authority ● Openness of communications; willingness to share information ● A belief that co-ordinating expertise from different people is better than going it alone; co-operation not competition ● Developing a network of individuals with shared visions and goals ● A strong sense of responsibility to co-workers ● Self-regulation of the network.

If you are fortunate enough to be in an organization which has that kind of structure and culture, the path will be relatively smooth, and you will be able to get on with the matter in hand without having to worry too much about organizational politics. On the other hand, if your organization has a long tradition of jealously guarded departmental autonomy, deriving from its history, then direct attempts to sell the virtues of 'information sharing' will be about as successful as telling a bunch of toddlers that it's nice to share their toys. Nor will proposals to introduce centralized management

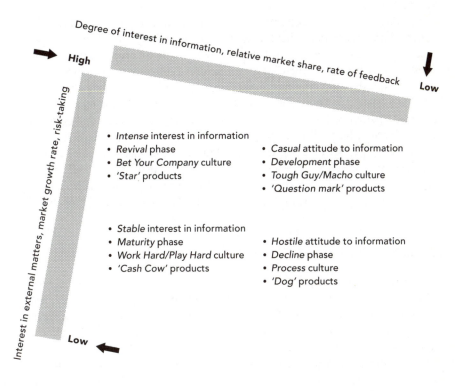

Based on Ginman (1987 with kind permission of the author

Figure 2.1
Linkages between CEO culture, company
culture, life cycle and business performance

of information have much luck. As Davenport et al (1992) put it, 'Unless the politics of information are identified and managed, companies will not move into the Information Age. Information will not be shared freely nor used effectively by decision makers ... [that] will take what politics always take, negotiation, influence-exercising, backroom deals, coalition-building, and, occasionally even war.'

In an organization where IT has a strongly entrenched position, and where top management sees information as synonymous with information technology, you won't get far without finding a management champion to educate about the distinction, and without trying to build a strategic alliance with IT and information systems colleagues in which both sides have something to gain. If, on the other hand, information has a bad name in the organization because it's been equated with IT and there have been some heavy losses from ill-judged and badly managed investments, it is no good going straight in with a proposal for a large investment in human resources for information management; once again you have to start by getting the distinction clear in management minds, and you will need to reinforce it by demonstrating some low-cost quick wins from doing something sensible with information.

If an organization is planning a major change in direction, the nature of the change is critical, and has to be taken into account in any information initiatives. As Marchand (1997) reminds us, it is particularly critical for organizations trying to change their orientation and/or culture to be aware of the information risks in the change and to seek to avoid them, as well as understanding how information can contribute positively to successful change. For example, an organization seeking to move towards innovation and changing to project-centred management for the purpose, runs the risk, as project teams disband, of losing useful information that could be exploited in future; for successful change, its information management will need a particular focus on conserving the memory of successes and failures and making it accessible for future use,

If we do not pay heed to these intangible but significant characteristics of the organization in which we are operating, the result may well be wasted effort, investment without visible return, disillusion, and loss of credibility for the people concerned; and the opportunity of doing something useful about information may be lost for years.

Questions about structure

We need to answer such questions as:
• What formal units is the organization divided into? companies, divisions, departments? • Do the main sub-divisions have a degree of autonomy, or is the organization highly centralized? • Where does the structure come on the line between hierarchy and network (*see* Figure 2.2, opposite) • What are its decision-making bodies, and what are their functions? • Does the organizational structure provide meeting places for interchange of information among people from different functions who contribute to the same process? • Who are the senior managers and what are their formal responsibilities? • How do their responsibilities relate to authority and accountability? • Who takes what decisions? • Who has power to override decisions? • Are there differences between what the organization chart depicts and the reality in day-to-day operations?

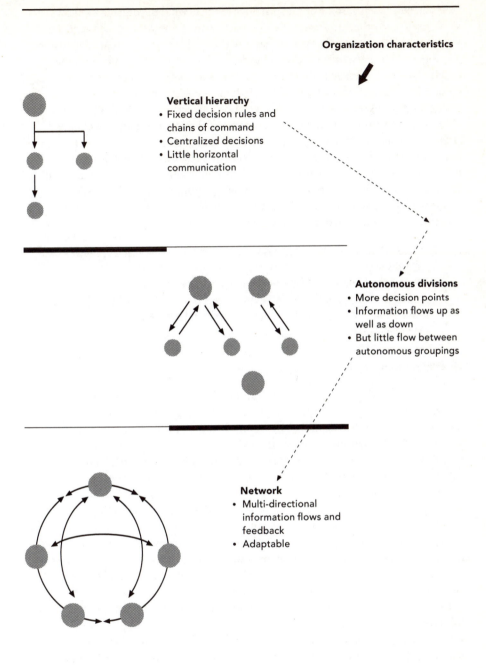

Organization characteristics

Vertical hierarchy
- Fixed decision rules and chains of command
- Centralized decisions
- Little horizontal communication

Autonomous divisions
- More decision points
- Information flows up as well as down
- But little flow between autonomous groupings

Network
- Multi-directional information flows and feedback
- Adaptable

Figure 2.2
Organizational structure and characteristics

As you will observe, some of the questions relate to what the organization says about itself, and others to what it does in practice and to how the two diverge. This is sometimes perilous territory; and that is why its exploration has to be undertaken by people with experience of the organization, and good standing in it, with the backing of senior management. It is part of the environment of human interactions, ideas and feelings against which initiatives for change have to be considered and evaluated. The degree to which the organization's structure matches its priority objectives can either smooth the path towards developing information policy and strategy, or make it very hard going. For example, an organization which combines a very hierarchical structure and slow decision processes with objectives that demand quick and flexible response to environmental changes will have difficulty in achieving a policy for information, or indeed for anything else. And if a policy is to be successfully introduced in such a situation, it will inevitably have structural consequences of the kind outlined by Horton (1987, p267):

> The introduction of the information management idea into organizations implicitly carries with it very substantial structural change consequences. For one, the integration of information technologies, operating information programs, and ongoing information services into a cohesive policy and operational framework implicitly means reshuffling people and blocks on the organization chart.

Questions about culture

The other essential questions we need to answer are not about what the organization says or does, but *how* it does it. As Eason (1988, p154) says, 'Any organization has its own, more or less explicit, culture and values; not what it does but the way that it does it.' The culture embraces the way the organization regards itself, the people who work for it, and its outside world; the way it presents itself to them; the way it treats them; and the 'stories' that are current in the organization to explain and account for what it does, and to help people make up for the deficiencies in what it provides to help them do their work. (For an interesting account of the significance of stories in organizational life and learning, *see* Brown and Duguid, 1994.) The culture therefore has a potent influence on how the organization values information, on the way it flows, and on how it is used, and so it will condition the resources it is prepared to devote to developing information policy and strategy, and affect the success of any such endeavours.

The questions that can elicit a picture of how the organization manages are of this kind:

- Does it have a Mission and Vision statement? How is it phrased? How do staff take it? Seriously? Cynically? As a bad joke? • Does it rely heavily on short-term contracts, and if it does, what provision does it make for job handover and transfer of knowledge? • Is its 'human resources' policy devoted to keeping people in their proper boxes and doing exactly what their job description says, or to encouraging initiatives, flexibility and development? • If it claims to encourage flexibility, does that mean in practice that it expects employees to accept every proposed change in work content and conditions without question? • Are there sharp boundaries between staff at different levels, or is collective and co-operative endeavour valued and rewarded? • Are there policies on staff development and training? If there are, to what are they directed, and are they implemented in practice? Do staff take part in formulating their own training needs and training plans? • How are industrial relations managed? Is the trend authoritarian, co-operative, or capricious? • Does the organization commit itself formally to openness and maximum access to information? If it does, how does this work out in practice? • Has it an ethical policy to guide its conduct towards the outside world and its own staff? • Is the main direction in which information travels from the top down, with responses going up through the prescribed channels? • Is lateral movement of information encouraged, or does rumour flourish in its absence? • Do different functions and departments keep themselves to themselves and clutch their knowledge tightly against prying eyes, or is there free interchange and cooperation between them? • Are professional staff encouraged to meet and discuss with colleagues in other organizations, with the expectation that they will have the good sense and loyalty to know where to exercise discretion; or are such exchanges frowned on?[2] • How does the organization take its decisions • Does it actually make use of the available information for assessing the various options, or does it look for information that will support the one it has already decided on? Does it draw on expertise and knowledge available among its staff? (Has it any means of knowing what *is* available?) • How good is the organization at knowing when to be cautious and when to be ready to take risks?

Resources for an investigation

One of the advantages of the approach recommended in this chapter is that it makes only a light demand on resources, and it is one where information managers can readily take an initiative. The analysis of information implications of objectives in particular is primarily desk research, requiring mainly thinking time. Knowledge of the organization and contacts with people in different parts of it are the main essentials for the consideration of organizational structure and culture; here the output from the analysis of what the objectives mean in terms of information can be used as the basis for discussions that should enrich understanding. While there is advantage in keeping the process fairly informal and low key, management support and understanding is essential from the start, and there is advantage in establishing protocols at this stage which will serve as a model for later more formal and extended projects.

The essential resources are:
• Commitment of top management to the defined purpose of the investigation (for example: 'To analyse the implications of key business objectives in terms of how the organization needs to use information and knowledge to achieve them, and to recommend appropriate action' • Person(s) of sufficient knowledge, experience, judgement and standing to carry it out • An adequate allowance of time for doing the job • Access to appropriate people and documents • Agreed methods of managing and reporting on the investigation.

2 There is plenty of research evidence over the last twenty years or so to show that businesses which encourage such exchanges are not only happier places to work, but also succeed better in innovation and compete more successfully. *See*, for example, Olson (1977), Koenig (1992) and Bowonder and Miyake (1992).

Readers should be able to judge what those resources would amount to in their own organization; in any case, at this stage it is wise to limit the number of people involved and to keep the time span short, because this is the start of a learning process, and it needs to be kept manageable. The qualities required of people who carry out this first investigation (and subsequent ones) are:
● Breadth of knowledge about the organization that extends beyond their own department or professional specialism ● Long enough experience in the organization to be aware of its character, and to be known to those from whom they will be seeking information ● Capacity to establish mutual professional respect with colleagues, to interact with them in a calm and courteous way, and to acquire information from them without wasting time ● Ability to analyse and synthesize information derived from both text and conversation ● Sufficient openness of mind to preserve them from prejudging and from interpreting what they are told in the light of their own preconceptions ● Ability to present the outcome in an accessible way, and to make a well-argued case for any recommendations arising.

Using the output

The output can be used as a basis for information auditing, or for initiating development of an information strategy, or for making a case for taking information use into account in any planned change initiative. And even if it appears to lead nowhere at the time, it is worth keeping on hand to bring forward on another occasion – one of the lessons of experience is that climates and views change, people who look like immovable obstacles go to exercise their talents elsewhere, and it is worth watching for opportunities to have another go. The next chapter looks at using the output as the foundation for information auditing.

Summary

● Before taking any decisions about information policy, we need to understand the organization for which it is to be designed: what it seeks to achieve, how it manages, how it sees itself and its outside world. (Rowlands', 1998, representation of information policy making on a national scale as 'a process of negotiation, bringing together competing value frames and resolving conflicts' is also valid at the organizational level.) ● That helps us to work out what the organization ought to be doing with information and knowledge, what the principles of its information policy should be, and the kind of systems and IT infrastructure it needs to support it.
● It also gives useful practical pointers for information auditing: where to start, what to look at, who to talk to, questions to ask. ● The organization's objectives make a useful starting point for asking and answering three questions:
1 What do the organization, and the people in it, need to *know* to achieve its objectives?
2 What *information* does it need to draw on to maintain the required knowledge?
3 How does the information need to flow and how do people need to *interact* in order to turn it into knowledge and act on it?
● Organizational structure and culture may favour developing information policy, or make it difficult ● Organizations which are seeking to make a major change in orientation need to pay special heed to the information risks entailed, and to under-

stand how information can contribute positively to successful change • This approach makes only a light demand on resources, and it is one where information managers can take initiatives, and establish their credentials for further development of information policy.

References

ABELL, A. (1996), 'The information professional in 1996', *Information management report*, January, 1–6.

ABELL, A. and WINTERMAN, V. (1993), *Information Culture and Business Performance. Literature Review and Feasibility Study*, HERTIS Information and Research, Hatfield: University of Hertfordshire.

BOWONDER, B. and MIYAKE, T. (1992), 'Creating and sustaining competitiveness: information management strategies of Nippon Steel Corporation', *International Journal of Information Management*, 12, 39–56.

BROWN, J. S. and DUGUID, P. (1994), 'Organizational learning and communities-of-practice: toward a unified view of working, learning and innovation', in H. TSOUKAS (ed) *New Thinking in Organizational Behaviour*, Oxford: Butterworth Heinemann.

DAVENPORT, T. H. et al (1992), 'Information politics', *Sloan Management Review*, Fall, 53–65.

DAVENPORT, T. and PRUSAK, L. (1998), *Working Knowledge*, Boston, MA: Harvard Business School Press.

EASON, K. (1988), *Information Technology and Organisational Change*, London: Taylor and Francis.

GINMAN, M. (1987), 'Information culture and business performance', *Iatul Quarterly*, 2 (2), 93–106.

HAWLEY COMMITTEE (1995), *Information as an Asset. The Board Agenda. Checklist and explanatory notes* and *Information as an Asset. The Board Agenda. A consultative report*, London: KPMG Impact Programme.

HORTON, F. W., Jr (1987), 'The impact of information management on corporate cultures', *Aslib Proceedings*, 39 (9), 267–274.

KOENIG, M. (1992), 'The importance of information services for productivity "under-recognized" and under-invested', *Special Libraries*, Fall, 199–210.

MARCHAND, D. (1997), 'Competing with Information: know what you want', *FT Mastering Management Reader*, July/August.

MARCHAND, D. A., KETTINGER, W. J. and ROLLINS, J. D. (2001), *Information Orientation*, Oxford: OUP.

OLSON, E. E. (1977), 'Organizational factors affecting information flow in industry', *Aslib Proceedings*, 29 (1), 2–11.

ORNA, E. (1990), *Practical Information Policies, how to manage information flow in organizations*, Aldershot: Gower.

ORNA, E. (1999), *Practical Information Policies*, Ed2, Aldershot: Gower.

OWENS, I. and WILSON, T. with ABELL, A. (1996), *Information and Business Performance. A study of information systems and services in high performing companies*, East Grinstead: Bowker-Saur.

ROWLANDS, I. (1998), 'Some compass bearings for information policy orienteering', *Aslib Proceedngs*, 50 (8), 230–237.

SILLINCE, J. A. A. (1994), Aldershot: Gower. management strategy for innovation and organizational design: the case of MPR2/JIT production management systems', *Behaviour and Information Technology*, 13 (3), 216–227.

SKYRME, D. (1992), 'Knowledge networking – creating wealth through people and technology' *The Intelligent Enterprise*, 1 (11/12), 9–15.

SYMON, G. et al (1992), 'The process of deriving requirements for a hospital information system, *Behaviour and Information*, 11 (3), 131–140.

This is a method for some first practical steps to arrive at a picture of 'What should be', and to start getting an understanding of how people in your organization actually experience using information in their work. I use it both in consultancy assignments in organizations, and in giving courses on information auditing. It's usually called mind-mapping, and goes back to methods developed by Tony Buzan and described in his *Mind Map Book*, 2000 (for a useful feature about recent applications in information work – some using Mind Manager software, others not – *see* Dale et al 2003).

The method is a good one for information professionals who want to take initiatives on information auditing or information strategy development, and equally useful where the requirement comes from the top of the organization. It can make the business of 'extracting meaning from objectives' rather less daunting than Tables 2.1– 2.3 may suggest. And it's a very cost-effective way of gathering ideas and experience. In consultancy, I've used it to start off the work of a core group who have responsibility for an information audit or information strategy initiative. It could equally be used by such a group before commissioning consultancy, to help them define a realistic brief. Taken in conjunction with the advice offered in the original chapter which you have just read, it should help to make a good start on the business of 'establishing the ground'.

The 'Post-it'®[1] method

Here's the essence of the 'Post-it ' method (the reason for the name will become apparent in a moment). As applied for this purpose, you build up two 'maps', around a framework that asks some relevant questions. All you need to start off the exercise is:

● A core group (which often consists of just one person to begin with; that can make a valid start, but the lonely pioneer should aim to bring in one or two allies as soon as possible) ● Basic knowledge of the organization's corporate objectives, key strategies, or whatever else it uses to define what it's in business for, enough experience of the organization to make sense of them, and curiosity that motivates the desire to learn more ● The map outlines – a copy for each person, and an enlarged copy which can be mounted on a large sheet of paper (flip-chart paper is fine) and stuck to a good big stretch of wall ● A few packs of *coloured* Post-it notes (3in by 3in is fine for size) – *not* the pale yellow that's the office standard, but the brightest possible. Don't ask me why they have to be bright colours; but it certainly seems to encourage thought and cheer people at the start of the proceedings!

1 All references to the term 'Post-it' in this book
should be understood as relating to the product
with this trademark.

The first map – a rough picture

The first map helps you consider the organization's key objectives and goals and what they imply in terms of how it should use the knowledge and information essential for achieving them. Figure 2.3 on the next page shows what it looks like.

And this is all you have to do: Put brief answers to the questions (with the question number on each, on Post-it notes); then post them on to the main map in the appropriate places. This is work that's best done individually, and it's important to get the answers straight on to the Post-its without too much pause for thought (not too difficult if you've done the preliminary reading and reflecting). It usually takes from half an hour to three-quarters for people to get their answers written and on to the collective map.

This is the point at which the core group can start operating as a group rather than individuals. All you have to do is look at what's there, and start talking about it. The exchange of ideas will probably lead to a few more notes on the map, and to organizing the responses as patterns of observations become apparent. Another half hour should be enough to get a first rough, top-level, picture of 'What should be'.

At the end of this session, it's worth taking a digital photograph or copy of the map for reference.[2]

A first picture of 'What is'

The next map starts drawing on the core group's experience of what actually happens – like a dummy run or rehearsal for the audit which will help ensure the group's confidence and competence in the real thing, just as physical actions like throwing or dancing can be performed more successfully if we 'image' them first. (*See* Figure 2.4 on p43 for an example of a map for this purpose).

The process of creating the 'What is' map is the same as for the 'What should be' one. The output can lead on to auditing workshops where groups from various areas of the organization map their answers to similar questions to give a set of pictures of how a sizeable sample of stakeholders experiences the organization's information culture and information behaviour, the tasks of finding and using information, information interactions, and the support – from people and from systems/IT – available for accomplishing them. (For more about running workshops, *see* pp69–72). And the maps from those workshops can be used to analyse experience and perceptions of the actual situation, for comparison with the 'What should be'.

2 I have found it useful to return to this first 'What should be' map at a later stage in audits, and refine it in the light of experience, to create a visual representation of how the organization would be using knowledge and information if it were doing everything it should to get full value from them in achieving whatever it's in business for. This can be used in various ways:
• During the actual audit with key stakeholders and work groups, for getting feedback and further refinements

• As an illustration in reports on the process, to help senior management and people who haven't been involved in the process to understand it
• In starting to plan a knowledge and/or information strategy, for developing objectives for the strategy.

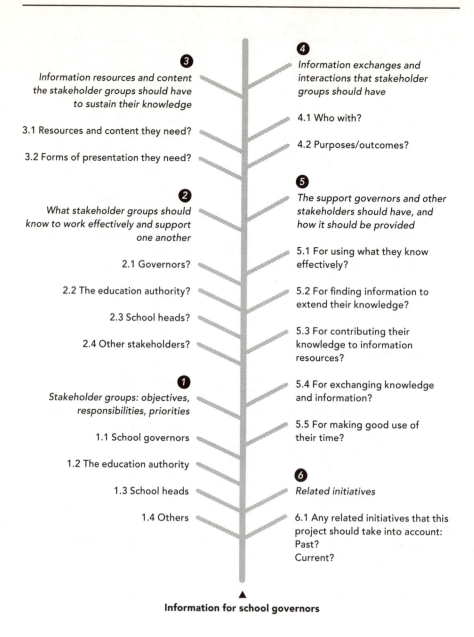

3

Information resources and content the stakeholder groups should have to sustain their knowledge

3.1 Resources and content they need?

3.2 Forms of presentation they need?

2

What stakeholder groups should know to work effectively and support one another

2.1 Governors?

2.2 The education authority?

2.3 School heads?

2.4 Other stakeholders?

1

Stakeholder groups: objectives, responsibilities, priorities

1.1 School governors

1.2 The education authority

1.3 School heads

1.4 Others

4

Information exchanges and interactions that stakeholder groups should have

4.1 Who with?

4.2 Purposes/outcomes?

5

The support governors and other stakeholders should have, and how it should be provided

5.1 For using what they know effectively?

5.2 For finding information to extend their knowledge?

5.3 For contributing their knowledge to information resources?

5.4 For exchanging knowledge and information?

5.5 For making good use of their time?

6

Related initiatives

6.1 Any related initiatives that this project should take into account:
Past?
Current?

▲

Information for school governors

Figure 2.3
School governors information audit
Mapping the issues – what should happen

③

The information resources stake-holders actually have access to

3.1 What resources and content are available?

3.2 Are they adequate? Shortcomings? Any missing resources?

3.3 Obstacles in the way of using them?

3.4 Who manages the resources?

②

What stakeholders actually know

2.1 Strengths?

2.2 Shortcomings, and their effects?

①

Stakeholder groups: objectives, responsibilities, priorities

1.1 How do they affect stake-holders' actions?

1.2 Differences or conflicts between priorities of different groups?

④

Information interactions and exchanges

4.1 Do stakeholders know what information they should exchange, and who with?

4.2 Does their organizational culture encourage or discourage interactions and exchanges?

4.3 Things that make interactions and exchanges difficult?

⑤

Support from the information environment

How well do the existing IT infrastructure and information services support stakeholders in:

5.1 Managing their knowledge and information effectively?

5.2 Accessing information resources and finding information they need?

5.3 Exchanging knowledge and information

5.4 Managing their time effectively?

5.5 How effective are the processes and products used in communicating information to the stakeholders?

▲

Information for school governors

Figure 2.4
School governors information audit
Mapping the issues – what is, as you experience it

Next steps

When the ground is established, and the initiators have got their ideas clear about what should happen next, they need to formalize them for starting off that next step. If they are seeking to 'sell' an information audit to management, they need to prepare a business case for it. If the initiative has come from the top, they should move on to a 'Project Initiation Document', or PID, which defines the objectives and scope of the project, how it will be done, the people involved in managing it, attendant risks and how they will be countered. Here is an example of the headings of a Project Initiation Document from an actual project – an information audit:

Example

Project Initiation Document:
Information Audit

Background

Project Definition
  Project objectives

Project scope

Method of approach

Project Deliverables and/or Desired Outcomes

Dependencies [groups, individuals, projects and processes on which the audit project depends or with which it has a relationship]

Interfaces [groups and individuals whom the audit will involve]

Assumptions [on which the project depends for success]

Initial Business Case [why the project should be undertaken;
balance of risks against benefits, costs and time/resource aspects]
  Risks and benefits

Project Organization Structure
  Project Board membership

Communications Plan [what to tell who, and how]
Project Plan/Strategy [overall policy for achieving required quality]

Initial Project Plan

Project Controls [progress reporting requirements, monitoring methods and how changes will be managed]

Initial Risk Log [risks currently identified and analysed]

Contingency Plans [for dealing with risks identified]

Project Filing Structure [paper and electronic files to be created and maintained]

References

BUZAN, T. with BUZAN, B. (2000), *The Mind Map Book* – Revised Edition, London: BBC Books.

DALE, A. et al (2003), 'Information: it's all in the mind', *Library+Information Update* 2 (4), 30–34.

Information auditing: from initial analysis to doing the audit

*Creative tension comes from seeing clearly where we want to be, our
'vision', and telling the truth about where we are, our current reality.
The gap between the two generates a natural tension ... an accurate
picture of current reality is just as important as a compelling picture
of a desirable future.*
–Senge, Peter, M. (1990)

> *How odd it is that anyone should not see that all observation must be
> for or against some view if it is to be of any service.*
> –Darwin, Charles. (1861) in a letter to Henry Fawcett

Not a new invention

Though it is only within the last decade or so that information auditing has started
to become popular with organizations, and to be the subject of articles and courses,
it is far from being a new invention. I first made an 'information audit' – though it
was not called that – more than 20 years ago, and reference to the term dates back to
at least 1982. A paper of that date by Taylor describes 'an audit of the formal information activities and their effect on the organisation' looking at how well they help
people to do their jobs. Taylor also says that it is essential to understand what the
organization does, its history, the place it occupies in its industry, and its market
share; to know about its customers, its clients, and its 'public'; and to be aware of
organizational 'dynamics' and 'culture' and how they influence the flow of information. And he says that eventually the audit should 'become an ongoing analysis of
the benefits and costs of each major activity'. In short, he presents a very far-sighted
view of information auditing, which is well ahead of some current rather simplistic
approaches to the topic.

Information audits are being done today in a wide range of businesses and organizations in the UK, from pharmaceutical firms, banks, and the health service,
to charities and cultural organizations such as museums. Their popularity probably
has something to do with the accountancy associations of the word 'audit', the
emphasis placed today on accountability and value for money in the matter of
information services, and the interest which large businesses are currently taking
in setting a value on information assets. That makes it important to have a clear
account of what the process entails, the resources it needs, and what organizations
can reasonably expect from carrying it through.

Definitions and what they imply

The brief definition which is becoming current in the UK today was developed
by the Information Resources Management Network of Aslib (the Association for
Information Management); it sums up the essentials in these terms:

> A systematic examination of information use, resources and flows, with a verification by reference to both people and existing documents, in order to establish the extent to which they are contributing to an organization's objectives.

We can expand this into a more detailed outline of what the audit examines:

1 The information an organization holds – on paper, in machine-readable form, and in the minds of the those who work for it – which can be turned into knowledge by people and applied in their work to meet its objectives
2 The resources for making information accessible to those who need to turn it into knowledge
3 The ways in which it uses information to further its objectives
4 The people who are involved in using information
5 The 'tools' it uses for doing things with information – from the simplest non-electronic indexes and filing systems to the most sophisticated computer applications and systems
6 The criteria it uses to assess the costs and values of information.

The definition has some important implications:

1 As the aim of the audit is to find out how the organization is using information to meet its objectives, the starting point has to be the organization's objectives, and what they imply about the information it needs to achieve them, and how it needs to use that information. Consideration of key business objectives should yield a basic statement of 'How It Should Be' in the matter of information and its use, which will form the reference point from which the audit starts. (Chapter 2 has dealt in detail with this process of defining what the organization should be doing with information.)
2 The audit process is a matter of asking appropriate questions to find out 'How It Actually Is' in respect of the matters outlined above
3 The output of the audit consists of the results of matching how it should be against how it is
4 Action on the output is a matter of interpreting the results, and deciding what to do to bring the organization's use of information closer to what its objectives require.

Unfortunately organizations do not always realize that it is dangerous to start an audit without the essential first step of looking at the information implications of their objectives. Not long ago I encountered an organization which had undertaken an audit without this preliminary, at a time when it was undergoing a good deal of pressure; when the audit was completed, they found themselves perplexed as to how to use the results because there was nothing against which they could match them.

Booth and Haines (1994) provide an example of a more thoughtful approach, with their account of an information audit of a regional health authority within the UK National Health Service. The strategy which they developed at the start was to:

1 Identify and review the corporate objectives of the authority
2 Decide what information is required to meet them
3 Do an information audit to determine if this information currently exists in the authority and, if so, to describe how it is currently used
4 Address any immediate information gaps and problems
5 Develop an information management policy to ensure appropriate resources,

organizational structures and training to meet the information requirements of the authority's corporate programme.

What can organizations expect from information auditing?

While information auditing can make a valuable contribution and bring benefits, there are dangers in undertaking it without knowing what one is letting oneself in for, so it is important to understand what organizations can reasonably expect to get out of doing it, what resources they need to put into it, and what they need to do with them if they are to get benefits. Any organization that initiates an information audit has to be prepared to think carefully about what information it needs, and what it needs to do with it in order to survive and succeed in meeting business objectives, ask the right questions to find out what information it actually has and how it is being used, and analyse the results honestly, and, finally, take appropriate action.

Nor is an audit something to be undertaken out of the blue and as a one-off operation. If the effort invested in it is to pay off, it has to be a stage in a carefully planned process. Organizations will get maximum value from information auditing if it is used as the starting point for an ongoing cycle of evaluating what they are doing with information, and learning from the process.

The benefits

The best way of looking at information auditing is as a key that can unlock the door to benefits. Because it gives us a map of what the organization is actually doing with information, and allows us to measure how well the reality matches what the organization ought to be doing with information, it provides a sound foundation for a range of benefits and initiatives, short- and long-term.

In the short term, the results of the audit allow:
● Attention to immediate threats, risk avoidance ● Cost savings from more rational management ● Quick gains from making information more accessible or usable for those who need it.

Over the longer term, the experience of the auditing process can promote valuable cultural changes, and provide a strong platform for policy initiatives:
● Enriched understanding of what information and knowledge mean for the organization – at the top, and throughout the organization ● Interaction and negotiation among the 'guardians' of information resources and the stakeholders in them ● Development of a strategy for managing knowledge and information ● Better use of information in supporting key business processes, and in initiating and responding to change ● Integrated management of the organization's complete range of information, supported by appropriate systems and technology ● Reliable assessment of the cost-effectiveness of information and its use, and of the proportion of the organization's total valuable assets which is contributed by the use of knowledge and information.

The audit process

There is as yet no standard for how to do information audits. Probably the way forward lies in establishing standards for what the audit should look at, while leaving organizations free to decide how they meet the standards, in the light of their definition of information and what they need to do with it, in relation to their key strategic objectives. At the same time, it is important that organizations should have access to relevant examples and case studies which they can draw on in planning their own audit. I am not convinced that the auditing model of the accountancy profession, with its certificates and signing off, is wholly appropriate here, because the purpose of information auditing is to establish a foundation for using information strategically, rather than to see that figures add up and things are being done 'correctly'. There are, however, other aspects of the practice of financial accounting which should be drawn on, especially meticulous attention to detail, and making the audit a repeated exercise.

While there is no 'standard procedure' (which worries some people unnecessarily), there is by now a fairly well-established common core of modern thinking about information auditing, which can be summarized in these terms:

1 *It matches:*
- What organizations are doing with information
  against
- What they should be doing with it in order to achieve their goals

2 *Things you need to know before starting an audit:*
- What the organization does and how it does it • Its market, customers, clients, public • Its culture – how it manages, how it sees itself, its staff, its role • Its present orientation – where it's trying to go now • Changes in orientation it seeks – where it wants to go in future

3 *Auditing looks at:*
- Information services, systems and products (including the often disregarded products which the organization uses to carry information about itself and its offerings to the outside world it depends on, seeks to serve or to influence; and those it uses to convey information internally) • How they support people in their work, in order to see how effectively information serves organizational objectives

4 *It provides a basis for:*
- Setting a value on the contribution that information makes to the organization
- Decisions about changes in ways of using information and benefits to be sought

5 *It should be an ongoing process, not a one-off*

6 *It is best managed in-house, though outside help is often useful.*

The process shown in Figure 3.1 is based on these ideas.

The first step – analysis of the information implications of what the organization is aiming to do – has been dealt with in detail in Chapter 2, so there will just be a brief reminder of it here. The rest of this chapter looks at stages 2–5 (that is, up to and including the process of doing the audit), identifies key issues, and suggests some approaches to them, some of which are exemplified in the case studies. The remaining stages – from interpreting the results and presenting them, through to deciding on action and setting up monitoring – form the subject of the next chapter.

A further point to make about this sequence of activities is that it represents a practical principle which can be applied for other purposes besides information auditing; readers will meet it again, in various guises, on the road to information policies and strategies.

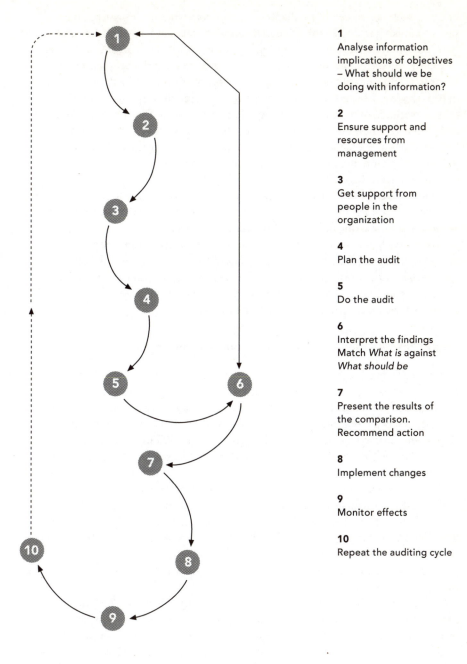

1
Analyse information implications of objectives – What should we be doing with information?

2
Ensure support and resources from management

3
Get support from people in the organization

4
Plan the audit

5
Do the audit

6
Interpret the findings Match *What is* against *What should be*

7
Present the results of the comparison. Recommend action

8
Implement changes

9
Monitor effects

10
Repeat the auditing cycle

Figure 3.1
The information auditing process

Step 1: Analyse the information implications of key business objectives

The first stage, as we saw from Chapter 2, starts from what the organization itself says it is seeking to do, as embodied in its mission statement, key business objectives, etc. From that, it derives a top level statement of what the organization needs to know to succeed in its aims, then from that an analysis of the information it needs to acquire and use in order to maintain its knowledge in a healthy state. This in turn serves as a basis for defining how people, inside the organization and in its outside world, need to interact in using information and applying knowledge. The end product is a first picture of 'what should be' in the way of using knowledge and information – a 'template' (*see* Figure 3.2 on opposite page) against which to match the 'what is' picture provided by information auditing.

It also gives invaluable clues to:
● What resources of information to look for ● Key people to talk to ● Information flows to seek ● Technological support needed ● Questions to ask ● How to ask them ● Useful starting points for audit pilots or projects.

Except in very small organizations, it is becoming the usual practice to identify projects which can be used to gain experience of the process at low risk and low cost, with the chance of gaining some practical demonstrable improvement. If this approach is adopted, the first top-level analysis can be taken to more detail for the areas in which auditing is going to be piloted.

Step 2: Ensure support and resources from management

Experience from all sides tells us that this step is a condition for success. If you don't ensure that top management understands what an information audit entails, and makes a firm commitment to it, there is little if any chance of success. So in the early stages a lot of time and effort needs to be devoted to initiatives and inter-actions with management. This requires a high level of skill in negotiation on the part of those responsible for the audit, together with deep understanding of the organization. The analysis of the information implications of organizational objec-tives can make a useful introduction to this process, and help in the basic informa-tion education of management, and that is why it is recommended as the first step. Corporate objectives can, after all, safely be assumed to be the creation of manage-ment, who are committed to them (and if not, they can hardly say so!), and so they make a solid foundation for the new ideas to which they have to be introduced.

The key points that top managers need to understand and give commitment to at the outset of the audit are:
● The objectives of the audit, both immediate and longer-term ● The long-term benefits to be expected, in terms of achieving key business objectives ● The scope proposed: is the audit to cover the whole organization, or parts of it, or particular activities or processes; is it to start with one or more pilot projects? ● The phases proposed: the audit plan should be based on realistic steps, with stopping points for evaluation and decision making ● The benefits from each phase: what the organi-zation can expect to gain from each step ● The timescale, expressed both in person days and total elapsed time to completion ● The deliverables, for example reports and presentations at the end of each phase ● The resources required.

What are we trying to do?

?
What do we need to know in order to do it

?
Who needs to know it

?
What information do we need to support the knowledge

?
What do we need to do with information to achieve what we are trying to do?

?
Who needs to do it and how

Questions we can answer from the organization's objectives

Figure 3.2
The answers to these questions make the output from the first stage: 'what should be'

The essential resources are:
● Support from top management ● People with knowledge, experience, judgement and standing to run the audit ● A proper time allowance for them to do the job ● Guaranteed access to people and documents ● A clear reporting line to the top level of decision making – the audit needs a management champion, who can be 'educated' by the people doing the audit, and who can in turn educate the rest of the senior management team.

Step 3: Get support from people in the organization

It is not only top management who need to understand what is being proposed. When they have given formal agreement on the points outlined above, it is essential that everyone in the organization who will be affected should be fully informed, and have the opportunity of asking questions, expressing any anxieties and receiving explanations. If this essential courtesy is not extended to them, and if the first they hear of it is a memo telling them to expect to be interviewed on a given day, they are more than likely to feel threatened, and will not make the essential contribution from their knowledge of their own work – and so the quality and reliability of the audit findings will suffer. The people who will be involved should also receive a guarantee that they will be able to take part in discussing the audit findings, so that they can contribute to the ultimate decisions. Without that, they will not be committed to change, and the investment in the audit is less likely to succeed and may well be wasted. Time given to this step is time well spent, because, as well as gaining commitment and interest for the audit, it helps people to set a value on their own knowledge, to understand the part that information plays in their work, and to appreciate their mutual responsibilities for interchanging it and negotiating about it.

Step 4: Planning the audit

Experience suggests that the lowest-risk and most productive approach is to select projects to start off the auditing process. This allows you to learn about doing the job in a more or less controlled environment, with minimal risks, and, if you pick your projects with care, to make a useful and quick contribution to improving information use, which gives tangible benefits.

Criteria for successful audit projects

There are some straightforward criteria for selecting potential audit projects. In the first place, look for areas where information has high strategic importance and where it has high potential for adding value. Here, once again, the preliminary analysis of the information the organization needs to achieve its aims makes a useful starting point. For each of the types of information identified, ask if it has any of the characteristics shown in Table 3.1 (*see* opposite page), and score its level of significance on each characteristic. The other criteria for potential projects are:
1 The area should have a clear boundary and not be too large
2 There should be potential for some 'quick wins'
3 There should be a fair proportion of staff in it who are information-aware.

An example: A project in an international information business

The area selected for an information audit pilot was the company's directory publishing operation. At that time the products were traditional printed volumes, but the company was planning to change its orientation towards electronic products. The audit looked at the processes of collecting, verifying and editing information for a range of directories, and at the technology in use to support the work; to see how well they were serving the objectives of maintaining the company's leading position in the market, and preparing for the move towards electronic products. The area was selected mainly because it seemed probable that organizational culture had an impact on the way in which information for the directories was collected. Details of organizations that figured in the directories were mostly collected by sales staff whose main job was selling these same organizations advertising space in the directories, and who therefore did not want to endanger good relations with customers by making too much fuss about the quality of the information

Characteristics of information	Score 5 = Absolutely critical 1 = Low significance				
Example: Customer information	5	4	3	2	1
Key strategic aims can't be achieved without it	●				
Essential for a desired change in the organization's orientation		●			
Essential work can't be done without it	●				
Legal requirements can't be met without it				●	
Essential for planning and monitoring processes				●	
It has to flow between people for a key process to take place	●				
Potential for use in cost saving or revenue generation		●			

Table 3.1
Identifying strategically important information

they provided. Many of the senior executives had themselves come up via sales; they understood the value of good relationships with customers who bought advertising, but had less idea of the damage potential of poor-quality information.

As a project, it met the criteria listed above: the quality of the information that went into the directories was critical for competitive success and for reputation; the relationships between the organizations that supplied information and the company were crucial; there was a clear boundary; there was potential for quick wins (especially via upgrading the support given to editorial staff by replacing some antiquated systems); and the nature of the work ensured that editors as a whole were information-aware.

In deciding on projects, it can also be useful to combine the judgement of the people responsible for the audit with a general or selective invitation to submit possible projects (for an example, *see* the Surrey Police case study, Orna, 1999). If people have something they particularly want to look at, their knowledge and motivation can be a strong advantage, though it will usually need to be supported by intensive training and help.

Key people

Who does the audit? This is a key decision; there are those who think it should be done by outside consultants, because they alone have a breadth of knowledge and expertise to which no-one inside the organization can aspire. My own view (as a consultant) is that this is expecting a lot of consultants (and rather more than most of us are likely to be able to deliver), and insultingly little of those who work in organizations. The more I see of the process, the more convinced I am that it should be managed and controlled from inside the organization, and carried through by people who work there. Outside help is certainly useful; appropriate consultants can offer experience of other audits, provide specialist support in such areas as questionnaire design or analysis, or training and support through regular discussion with the audit team of problems and progress, but the invaluable component is the knowledge which people have of their own organization. And they are the ones who will have to live with the results and put them to use.

The core audit team who will be responsible for managing the audit should be chosen for their strategic understanding of the organization's business, and their ability to interact with a wide range of people – especially to listen to them; and they should be of good standing in the organization. It is essential to ensure that they all have the same understanding of what they are doing – so the programme should provide for frequent team meetings, careful initial training, and feedback. Booth and Haines (1994) give an account of very thorough training for an information audit in the health service. If the audit is being carried out as a series of projects, with the work on each done by a group which has a particular interest in the area, it will usually be necessary to pay particular attention to 'induction training' to help them get to grips with the underlying concepts, and with the management aspects of doing the job. They will need support from the core audit team in this, to ensure that all projects run on comparable lines so that the results can be treated with the same level of confidence – especially important where projects cover different stages of the same process, or gather evidence on it from different parts of the organization. In large and diverse organizations, it may also be necessary to have a steering group to oversee the whole audit process.

None of this, however, should deter small organizations which can afford only the time of one person for information auditing. If the person has the appropriate qualities, and is freed for the period of the audit from at least a proportion of their normal workload, it is a feasible undertaking. Of course the scale has to be limited, and the investment of effort targeted, but that is no bad thing, and at least the one-person audit manager has minimal problems of project administration and none at all in team building and supervision (for an example of a successful one-person audit. *see* the Ministry of Agriculture, Fisheries and Food case study in Orna, 1999, p274).

Who do the auditors need to talk to? There are two main groups with whom the people carrying out the audit will need to interact; and again, the analysis of the information implications of objectives should give pointers to them:
1 People who are given responsibility by the organization for being 'guardians' (some organizations call them 'stewards') of specific kinds of information, or for managing it on behalf of the organization, together with the managers to whom they have ultimate responsibility. For example:
● Those who have responsibility for acquiring, making accessible, and disseminating certain kinds of information ● Those whose permission has to be asked for using particular forms of information ● Those who have the right to update and change databases.
2 'Stakeholders' in information, that is, the people who have a legitimate need for particular kinds of information in their work, and whose voice therefore needs to be heard in decisions about it.

Methods

A variety of methods can be used in information auditing. They include: study and analysis of documents, and of databases used in conveying information; observation of how people carry out information tasks; structured interviews; informal meetings of work groups to identify key problems; questionnaires; mapping and other forms of visual representation; and Soft Systems Analysis (*see* Chapter 4, p75 for an example). Table 3.2 (pp56–57) suggests where they are useful, and what to watch out for.

The choice of methods is again something on which sound knowledge of the organization and its culture should be brought to bear. Methods need to be worked out very carefully in advance; the people applying them should have appropriate training and practice, and professional advice should be sought if necessary on such matters as developing and testing questionnaires, interviewing techniques, and software for analysing results or presenting data visually (for examples of the use of appropriate software to support audits, see the case studies of the Australian Securities Commission and the University of North London, in Orna, 1999, pp197 and 349). If your organization has specialists in any of these areas, it can help to spread understanding and win allies to consult them – we all like to have our expertise recognized, and we feel kindly towards colleagues who appreciate it. At this stage in preparing for the audit, it is essential to take basic decisions on the kind of analyses to be made of the results; simplest and strongest is probably the best advice. Information auditing is more craft than scientific research. Better a limited set of statements and a small number of correlations in which it is possible to have reasonable confidence than a complex analysis of dubious reliability which acts as an obstacle to interpretation and action.

It is essential to remember that information auditing is not just a technical task. Whatever methods we use must, of course, be reliable and properly applied, but doing an audit is not just a matter of counting and statistics; it is primarily a job of interacting with people, in some quite sensitive areas, so selection and preparation of the audit team, preliminary presentation to people in the organization, and all subsequent interactions with them deserve the utmost attention. So planning needs to include how and when progress reports will be given.

If, on the other hand, you wish to kill an audit stone dead, here are four simple steps for doing it:

1 Try to cover too much at once
2 Ask more questions than you need
3 Make sure the audit team don't share the same view of what they're doing
4 Make sure that the people on the receiving end don't understand the purpose.

Step 5: Finding out

We come, at last, to actually 'doing the audit'. This is the stage when we ask a parallel set of questions to those asked at the start in order to define what knowledge and information the organization needs to achieve its objectives, and how it needs to use them (*see* Figure 3.3, p58).

There are five key areas, which are relevant to any audit project:

1 Information resources (both content and 'containers')

Methods	What they are useful for
Analysis of documents and databases	Useful preliminary before taking up people's time with interviews or questionnaires Good basis for deciding what questions to ask
Observation	Useful for spotting where systems or presentation of information make tasks difficult. NB Get permission from the people you are going to observe and make sure they're happy to be watched.
Trying things out for yourself	Useful for spotting possible obstacles to getting at and using information that people need in their work; a good basis for deciding on questions to ask
Structured interviews	Useful for tapping into people's knowledge, learning how they use information in their job, how information flows, difficulties in getting/using what they need. *I'm not convinced of the value of working to a fixed script in the information auditing situation; probably a more informal structure which covers the main points but allows the people involved to make their own decisions will produce better results.* NB Give people an outline of the topics of interest beforehand; meet them in their own territory if possible; let them take the lead in talking; ask them about what they do and what they need to know to do it, *not* about what information they use.
Informal meetings of work groups	Useful for identifying problems as they perceive them in the area of the audit Helpful as a basis for deciding on questions and where to address them
Questionnaires	Use with care, and don't try to find out more than you can analyse. Useful for quantitative data, and for gathering experience and views on key topics. Keep them short; make them easy to fill in without error (you'd be surprised at how many wrong ends to a stick respondents can find) and easy to extract data from for analysis. Plan them in co-operation with whoever will do the analysis. For qualitative information use 5-point scale with meaningful phrases to describe them (informal meetings should yield some pointers to these). Keep open-ended response to a minimum

Table 3.2
Methods and where they are useful

Methods	What they are useful for
Mapping and other visual methods from strings of words	Simple visualizations of the audit area; information resources in it; the immediate and wider organizational context, and the 'outside world'; and information flows are helpful in disentangling the reality They can be supported by summarized answers to such questions as: • What's in this information resource? • Who's its guardian? • Who are the stakeholders? • What comes in? • Who from? • What goes out? • Who to?

Table 3.2 (end)

2 Guardians and stakeholders
3 Information flow and interactions
4 Technology and systems to support the use of information
5 How the cost-effectiveness of information is assessed.
For each area, there are essential questions which the audit has to seek an answer; the basic form of these questions is outlined below, but the detail, the emphasis, and the way in which they need to be asked is the critical element, and you have to make your own decisions in the light of your knowledge of your own organization.

Another set of decisions at this stage concerns how to record the findings; they need to be taken before the finding out begins, not while it is in progress. The aim is to make it easy to record accurately and economically, to minimize effort in preparing reports on the findings, and to make them intelligible to the people they are presented to. Since the whole purpose of information auditing is to allow us to match what the organization *should* be doing with information, and what it *is* doing, so as to see how well it is contributing to meeting its objectives, the recording of findings should aim to make the comparisons easy. If the first stage of analysing the information implications of the organization's objectives has resulted in a formal statement, the sections of that should be used as a guide to developing the materials for recording audit findings.

Where you are looking for quantitative results that lend themselves to being turned into tables or graphs, plan the recording forms so that they make it easy to extract and key data from them. For recording qualitative results about people's experience or opinions (from interviews or questionnaires) use five-point scales as far as possible, and limit open-ended questions to where they can throw useful light and yield telling quotations. Where the audit involves observing processes or systems, or examining documents, establish checklists of critical criteria related to the purpose for which people use them in their work, and identify how well they support people in doing the job.

Pre-test everything you plan to use in recording:
◉ Is it understandable for the people who will be doing the recording? ◉ Is it easy

?
What do we need to know in
order to do it

?
Who needs to know it

?
What information do we need
to support the knowledge

What are we trying to do?

?
What do we need to do
with information to achieve
what we are trying to do

?
Who needs to do it and how

Questions we can answer from
the organization's objectives

Questions we can answer from
the information audit

?
What do we actually know

?
Who actually knows it

?
What information do we
actually have

?
What are we actually doing
with it

?
Who is doing it
How

Figure 3.3
The original set of questions (*see* Figure 3.2) and
the parallel 'what do we actually know?' set

for them to fill in? • Is it easy to extract data from it, or to analyse? • Is it easy for people participating in the audit to understand, without ambiguity? • Does it allow people to answer easily and without errors?

If you find anything that fails these tests, amend it until it passes; otherwise what you get from the audit may be unreliable.

Key questions on information resources

We have to be prepared to find information resources in every part of the organization, not just in formal repositories like libraries or information systems, and not just in those functions where people spend a lot of time reading, writing, or interacting with computers. The touchstone for identifying information resources is:

> Is this something which holds information that people need to apply in their work, to achieve their, and the organization's objectives?

The things that meet this criterion will obviously differ according to the business of the organization; allowing for that, they will include such resources as: • Customer records • Information from and about suppliers • Information about operating budgets • Financial results • R&D reports, from its own operations, and from outside • Competitor information: how they are doing financially; what they are producing • The information products of the organization itself, for the world outside, and for the internal audience of its own staff • Information from and about its constituency, its market, its target audience, or its clients • Information about subject areas of importance to its work, for example: the industry sector it belongs to; the education system; science and technology; processes, materials, plant, or equipment • Information from the monitoring of its production processes • Information about the broader environment in which it operates: the economy, legislation, government and European Union regulations, social change, demography, etc.

In the wording of this list, I have been careful to avoid referring to the particular physical forms in which information may be embodied. It could be in books, periodicals, internal reports, market research reports, brochures or correspondence, or held in machine-readable form in databases, but for the purpose of identifying information resources the form is irrelevant, though it can become relevant later on when we start evaluating how well resources serve the users and their purposes. Readers may also notice that the list does not treat as separate categories information which comes from outside and that which originates inside the organization. This too is deliberate. Though enlightened organizations set themselves the aim of being able to search all their diverse information resources as if they were a single database, many organizations still needlessly hamper their work by not letting the left hand of external information see what the right hand of internal information is doing. They organize their databases or collections of material according to where the content originates from, keep them physically separate, use different ways of structuring them and looking for information – and in the process lose the chance of letting them interact and illuminate one another. Of course it is essential to be able to identify where particular pieces of information come from, and to group things from a specific source physically. But it is a perverse waste of potential value to put large obstacles in the way of finding all the relevant information on any issue, regardless of whether it came from outside or inside.

The basic questions about information resources are:
● What are they? ● Where are they? ● Who is responsible for them? ● What kind of information do they contain? ● How do the people who manage them define the users and the way in which they are used? ● What do the users themselves say? ● Are there other people who could make good use of this resource who o Don't know about it? o Know about it, but don't have access to it?

Key questions about guardians and stakeholders

The information audit brings us into personal contact with the people who are entrusted by the organization with managing the resources of information, and with those whose work needs make them interested parties – guardians and stakeholders. It provides the opportunity of mapping the lines of control, the placings of focal points for information management within the organization structure, and the interrelation between them. In large organizations, it is quite likely that services and systems for handling information will have developed separately within autonomous companies or divisions; alternatively, the parent organization may have set up a range of separate central services covering different functions or physical forms of information. It is also important to find out the division or department in which 'information resource entities' are located, the source of their funding, and the provision – if any – for formal or informal links and information exchange between them.

At the level of 'organizational culture', it is necessary also to be sensitive to which grouping or individual is accepted to be 'top dog', where they stand in relation to information resources and their management, and how willingly or otherwise the other 'dogs' concede the leadership. This is important, because if changes are recommended as a result of the information audit, the power structure of the present management of information must be taken into consideration.

The questions to be asked about guardians and stakeholders are:
Guardians
● What is their place in the organization's structure? ● What are their reporting lines? ● What is their work specialism? ● What training/experience have they in information management? ● What are their contacts o With the guardians of other information resources? o With stakeholders in the information they manage? ● What knowledge do they have of the work of other guardians, and of stakeholders?
Stakeholders
● Who are they? ● How do they use information in their jobs? ● What contacts do they have with the guardians of the information they use? ● Are there information resources that would be useful to them which they o Can't get at? o Don't know about?

Key questions about information flow

When we investigate what people do with information, we quickly become aware that it is a fluid element – its nature is to flow (though it also sometimes goes straight down the drain, or gets dammed up in stagnant ponds, or disappears underground never to emerge again). But it is not just something that goes through the plumbing; human minds interact with it, they consume it and transform it into knowledge; it is also a means by which people interact with one another and exchange ideas. Without that kind of interaction, information would be of little use to the organization, and would generate no changes or advances. (*see* Table 2.3, pp27–32).

The essential things we need to find out are: Who gives what information to whom? and how does the information people get match what they need in order to do their job? So the questions to ask people in the audit are:
• What information do you receive as part of your job from: o People inside the organization? o People outside the organization? • How does what you receive match what you need to do your job? • What information do you give as part of your job to: o Other people in the organization? o People outside the organization? • What contact do you have with the people o to whom you give information? o from whom you receive it? • Are you able to discuss information needs with them?

Key questions about technology

Throughout this book, readers will notice that IT is always considered after information content, information use, and the people who use information. That sequence is a deliberate choice, because it is the logical order. We have to know what material we want to work on, and what we want to make with it, before we can decide what are the right tools for the job (and it is worth remembering once again that even today not all tools are, or need to be, electronic ones). Of course it is true that information technology is qualitatively different from earlier technologies because of its potential for adaptive interaction with its users, intertwining with human thought, and enabling new ways of thinking – but the first steps to interaction still have to be initiated by humans. And the humans who do the work that the technology is meant to support are the ones who should make the most important contribution to specifying what the technology should be able to do to help them. These ideas are more widely accepted today than when I first wrote about this topic (Orna 1990), but there are still too many examples of disastrous 'collusion' among those who design and market hardware and software, those who make the decisions to buy, and those who manage IT and information systems, in which all the parties are unaware of:
• The significance of information for the organization • What it really needs to do with information • Basic principles of managing information.

The information audit can be a first step towards a policy for IT and systems that not only avoids the disasters of ignorance but capitalizes on the knowledge resources of those who work for the organization. The aim at this stage is not just to make an inventory of IT and systems, but also to see how people use them for all aspects of managing information resources throughout the organization.

The essential questions about the technology centre on how it supports people in using information in their work:
• How is it being applied in doing things with information? • How appropriate is it for the tasks people have to use it for? • How easy is it to use? How reliable is it? • What say did the users of particular systems have in specifying what they should do for them? • How compatible is it with other systems being used? • Who makes the purchasing decisions? • Who manages the technology? • What are the interactions between them and the people who use it to manage information?

Key questions about how the costs and value of information are assessed

There are those who think an information audit should provide an estimate of actual cost and value of information to the organization. It seems to me that this represents an attempt to go too far too fast, because this is a very complex area (*see* M'Pherson, 1994 and Orna, 1996, for an overview). But an audit *can* usefully find out what the organization's current practice is in this respect.

• What kind of information costs are taken into account? o Purchase of equipment, actual information? o Staff costs? • Is any account taken of costs saved by having and using information, for example in staff time, risk avoidance? • How are the costs and benefits of proposed information investments assessed? • Does the organization try to evaluate information resources in relation to how much and how well they contribute to key business objectives? • Does it value information in such terms as those proposed by Burk and Horton (1988)? o Quality (for example accuracy, comprehensiveness, relevance)? o Utility (for example accessibility, ease of use, quality of presentation)? o Impact on productivity (for example contribution to decision making, product quality, time-saving)? o Impact on effectiveness (for example contribution to new markets, customer satisfaction)? o Impact on financial position (for example cost reduction or saving, substitution for more expensive inputs, increased profits, return on investment)? • Does it recognize 'intellectual capital' (the knowledge and know-how of those who work for it, their ideas and initiative) as a driving force in its business?

It has to be said that not many organizations show up strongly here, but the subject is increasingly engaging the interest of decision makers in business who are aware that information and knowledge probably have a large potential value, though ideas about how to set a figure on it are mostly rather vague. So the audit can bring a degree of clarity by at any rate establishing what the organization's actual practice is, and that in turn will make an essential basis for any future attempt to establish the value contribution of knowledge and information (see Chapter 7, pp131–135 for further consideration of this topic).

Summary

Having followed the audit process through to the point where the job of finding out is completed, it is time to take a break, to summarize the story so far, and to look ahead to the next stages, which are the subject of Chapter 4.

• The information audit is a process of matching what should be with what is.
• So before starting, we need to establish what information resources the organization should have, and what it should be doing with them • Don't start without A) support and guaranteed resources from the top, B) understanding from the people who will be affected • It's not a once-for-all job; it needs to be a regularly repeated process • In itself it can bring some immediate benefits, and it can unlock the door to longer-term ones, by providing a solid basis of knowledge for policy initiatives • It is best done in stages, or by a series of projects – to minimize risk and maximize learning from experience • It should be managed from within, drawing on the organization's own knowledge of itself, not handed over to outsiders to carry out • Information auditing is a process of interacting with people, not just a technical exercise.

Information strategy in practice

References

BOOTH, A. and HAINES, M. (1994), 'Information audit: whose line is it anyway?', *Health Libraries Review*, 10 (4), 224–232.

BURK, C. F., Jr and HORTON, F. W., Jr (1988), *Infomap: a complete guide to discovering corporate information resources*, Englewood Cliffs NJ: Prentice Hall.

DARWIN, C. (1861), In a letter to Henry Fawcett, 1861, quoted in Gould, S. J. (1997), *Dinosaur in a Haystack*, London: Penguin Books, p148.

M'PHERSON, P. K. (1994), 'Accounting for the value of information', *Aslib Proceedings*, 46 (9), 203–215.

ORNA, E. (1990), *Practical Information Policies, how to manage information flow in organizations*, Aldershot: Gower.

ORNA, E. (1996), 'Valuing information: problems and opportunities', in D. Best (ed) *The Fourth Resource: Information and its Management*, Aldershot: Aslib/Gower.

ORNA, E. (1999), *Practical Information Policies*, (Ed2), Aldershot: Gower.

SENGE, P. M. (1990),' The leader's new work: building learning organisations', *Sloan Management Review*, 32 (1), 7–23, 9.

TAYLOR, R. (1982), 'Organisational information environments', in G. P. Sweeney (ed) *Information and the Transformation of Society*, Amsterdam; Oxford: North-Holland Publishing Company.

Reading list

DAVENPORT, T. H., et al (1992), ' Information politics', *Sloan Management Review*, Fall, 53–65.

DAVENPORT, T .H. (1993), *Process Innovation. Reengineering work through information technology*, Boston, MA: Harvard Business School Press.

DIMOND, G. (1996), 'The evaluation of information systems: a protocol for assembling information auditing packages', *International Journal of Information Management*, 16 (5), 353–368.

DRUCKER, P. (1995), 'The information executives truly need', *Harvard Business Review*, January–February, 55–62.

FARBEY, B. et al. (1995), 'Evaluating business information systems: reflections on an empirical study', *Information Systems Journal*, 5, 235–252.

GINMAN, M. (1987), 'Information culture and business performance', *Iatul Quarterly* 2 (2), 93–106.

HAWLEY COMMITTEE. (1995), *Information as an Asset. The Board Agenda. Checklist and explanatory note*, KPMG Impact Club.

HAYNES, D. (1995), 'Business process reengineering and information audits', *Managing information*, 2 (6), 30–31.

HAYWARD, R. and BROADY, J. E. (1995), 'The role of information in the strategic management process', *Journal of Information Science*, 21 (4), 257–272.

HERGET, J. (1995), 'The cost of (non)-quality: why it matters for information providers', *FID News Bulletin*, 45 (5), 156–159.

M'PHERSON, P. K. (1995), 'Information mastery', *Aslib Proceedings*, 47 (3) , 109–116.

MARSHALL, J. (1993), *The Impact of Information Services on Decision Making: some lessons from the financial and health care sectors*, Information Policy Briefings No.1, British Library Research and Development Department.

ORNA, E. (1996), 'Information auditing', *Singapore Libraries*, 25 (2), 69–82.

REUTERS BUSINESS INFORMATIONπ(1994), *To Know and not to Know: the politics of information*, Based on research conducted by Taylor Nelson AGB.

REUTERS BUSINESS INFORMATION (1995), *Information as an Asset: the invisible goldmine*, Based on research conducted by the Industrial Research Bureau.

ROBERTSON, G. (1994), 'The information audit: a broader perspective', *Managing information*, 1 (4), 34–36.

Setting the terms of reference

This is an example of a statement of the terms of reference for an audit project. It was prepared by the information manager responsible for the audit at the beginning of the project, so that everyone concerned should start with a clear understanding of the purpose of the audit, how it would be run, and the responsibilities of all concerned in it. The final part of the document is particularly important: it sets out the risks to which the project may be subject, and the steps taken to protect it against them – it's essential to bring things like this into the open at the start, rather than being ambushed by them when it's too late to safeguard the project against them.

Readers who work in government will be acquainted with documents of this kind; if treated as an opportunity rather than a bureaucratic formality, they are an excellent discipline. And the practice of setting terms of reference and getting management signed up to them can save trouble later – audits can be derailed and fail to fulfil their potential because they didn't have clearly agreed terms of reference, and that allowed other tasks and objectives, unrelated to the original project, to be 'slipped in' and drive it off course.

Pilot Information Audit
Project Terms of Reference

1 Project statement

1.1 Background

[Why the organization decided to undertake the audit; its key strategic aims in relation to knowledge and information]

1.2 Project Goal
The Information Audit will establish:
Where knowledge and information are most critical for good performance in the organization
Shortcomings in availability, use and exchange of knowledge and information and how they may affect the organization's work.
Examples of good practice.
Recommendations to overcome knowledge and information deficiencies and capitalize on opportunities.

1.3 Timeframe
Final report on the pilot audit by 30 11 2002

2 Project Governance

2.1 Project Sponsor
The project sponsor is responsible for:

Guaranteeing project resources for the project team

Assisting with pilot interviews

Supporting and communicating information about the pilot information audit

Providing comment on draft project documentation

Setting up the Project Board

2.2 Project Board

The project board will be responsible for:

Setting the direction of the project

Monitoring progress against the project plan; responding to reports from the project manager and agreeing deviations from the plan

Providing resources; ensuring the project team have adequate people/time/money available for the project

Signing off project products;

eg Interim Project Initiation Document, plan and reports

eg Final project report

The role of the project board will be to:

Provide and disseminate general support for the pilot information audit

Guarantee and commit resources to the project

Turn around project documents in good time

Attend project board meetings

Act as trouble shooters if required

Programme of Project Board Meetings

2.3 Project Team

Project Manager

Project Administrator

Project Consultant

Project Member (assisting with Interviews)

Project Supporter (assisting with document drafting and interviews)

The Project Manager is responsible for:

Preparing project documentation:

Project Initiation Document

Briefing and communications notes

Risk register

Interim reports to the project board and sponsor

Interview invitation letters

Interviewing key stakeholders with the help of the consultant, project sponsor and project member

Running audit workshops for pilot directorate staff with consultancy help

Weekly progress reporting to the project sponsor

Reporting to the project board

Managing the project administrator

Keeping the project supporter up to date with project methods and progress

Ensuring the project schedule is kept to

Final report

The Project Administrator is responsible for:
Preparing project material including:
Current knowledge and information map from the Information
audit workshop
Audit project plan and schedule
Co-producing the information audit briefing note
Interview recording form
Project board minutes
Distributing project materials to the appropriate people
Organising interview dates and booking rooms
Arranging the project board meetings and distributing relevant
papers/reports
Helping to organise the workshops
Keeping track that the schedule is being kept to and acting to
keep it on time

The Project Consultant is responsible for:
Running a two day pilot audit workshop to prepare the methodologies and
project plan and schedule
Assisting the project manager with the first pilot interview and workshop
Providing comment on draft project documentation
Providing consultancy work as requested by the project manager

The Project Member is responsible for:
Assisting with interviews as and when time allows
Providing comment on draft project documentation

The Project Supporter is responsible for:
Bringing experience and knowledge to the team on previous related
information management projects
Providing comment on draft project documentation

3 Key Stakeholders

[List, with job title, level of support likely to be given to project,
involvement in related projects, for each key stakeholder]

4 Project Risks

Risk: Lack of project resource
Impact: The project will fall behind schedule, or at the worst, fail
Advance counter-measure: Guarantees from project board and sponsor that
sufficient resource, time and money required by the project will be given
Risk: There may be hostility towards the project
Impact: Staff will not co-operate in sharing their knowledge and information
Advance counter-measure: The project is being communicated in a positive,
new way, highlighting the benefits of the audit to participants
Risk: Recommendations resulting from the audit are ignored
Impact: The organization will not benefit from the time and resources used to
ensure that its staff make the best use of the knowledge available to them

Advance counter-measure: Recommendations must be practical and easily implemented. A good relationship with the departmental sponsors must be formed to bring participating departments 'on side'

Communicating with audit participants

Key stakeholders

If you get off on the wrong foot in this, it's impossible to recover and the effects will threaten the success of the whole audit. The essentials are:
• Establish a standard definition of the audit project and its aims, which will be used throughout the organization in all communications about it from start to finish, so that you maximize the chance of common understanding • Approach the key stakeholders whose contribution is the first you will seek in good time and courteously; give assurance of confidentiality, and of not taking too much of their valuable time • Explain what's being asked of them; give them advance notice of the key topics on which you will seek their views.

Here are examples from the audit described in the last section:

Example

An email to key stakeholders who have been invited and have agreed to interviews:

Dear * * * * *

Thank you for agreeing to be interviewed as part of the pilot Information Audit project. The interview will only take half an hour of your time, but will enable us to build up a picture of the areas where knowledge and information are critical to your business, and of your current approaches to creating, managing and sharing information and knowledge.

The attached letter provides an explanation of the project and your involvement as a key stakeholder. The second document provides a list of the general topics and possible questions we would like you to consider in the interview.

I look forward to meeting you.

(Project Manager)

Explanation of project
Pilot Information Audit Interviews

This project forms part of the organization's Knowledge Management pro-gramme, whose overall aim is to ensure that it makes the best use of all the knowledge its staff possess, acquire and create through their work, and that it uses its resources of information productively to support all its knowledge activities – externally and internally.

The first stages of the project are concerned with building up a picture of the areas where knowledge and information are critical for our business, and of our current approaches to creating, managing and sharing information and knowledge. As we do this, we will also identify good practice and deficiencies in our ability to use our knowledge and experience, as well as opportunities for improvement. To gather this information, we are conducting interviews with a range of key stakeholders, after which we will extend our information gathering through workshops.

Thank you for agreeing to be interviewed; we look forward to meeting with you. The general topics that we would like to consider in the interview are set out in an attached document. The specific aspects we discuss will be those relevant to your particular role. You are assured that any information or views given in interviews will be presented in our reports in a way that does not attribute them to any individual.

Topics on which the views and experience of key stakeholders are sought, with particular reference to their own work and that of their department

The Organisation
● How its business objectives influence your department's use of knowledge and information ● Its policy for using knowledge and information ● Related projects to the present one: past and current ● Key issues a) affecting this project, b) that it should help to resolve ● The extent to which organizational culture supports communication/exchange of knowledge and information; learning from experience, including errors and failures

Knowledge and information needs
● The knowledge and know-how which are essential for acting successfully in your work for the organization ● The resources of information needed for keeping that knowledge up to date

How the needs are met
● The most important information resources (internal and external) actually used to keep knowledge up to date, and their quality ● Any problems in a) locating sources for required information, b) finding the specific information within them

Information environment
● The technology tools available to support getting, using, creating and communicating information ● The information services available ● The effectiveness of the support given by tools and services

Information processes and products
● The information resources which your department is responsible for managing ● The people responsible for them; how they manage them; their qualifications for information management; training and support available to them ● Communication and exchange of essential information across directorate boundaries and between people doing different jobs within the same directorate; the kinds of information communicated, and the medium. The quality of what is received ● Gaps and barriers that affect the flow of essential knowledge and information

Desirable changes
● Changes that would enable more effective use of knowledge and information in your department's work

Information strategy in practice

Other participants

A broader cross section of people needs to be drawn into the audit after reflecting on the contribution from key stakeholders. In the pilot audit described above, it was decided to run workshops for a range of people in the pilot department for this purpose, and to use the mapping method described in Chapter 2.2 – partly to meet a tight time target, partly to try out the method. Here are examples of communication with the workshop participants.

Example

email invitation to a workshop

Dear * * * * *

You are invited to a workshop in connection with the pilot information audit which is being carried out in * * * * * Department.

This project forms part of the organization's Knowledge Management programme, whose overall aim is to ensure that it makes the best use of all the knowledge its staff possess, acquire and create through their work, and that it uses its resources of information productively to support all its knowledge activities – externally
and internally.

The first stages of the project are concerned with building up a picture of the areas where knowledge and information are critical for our business, and of our current approaches to creating, managing and sharing information and knowledge. As we do this, we will also identify good practice and deficiencies in our ability to use
our knowledge and experience, as well as opportunities for improvement.

So far the audit team has conducted interviews with a range of key stakeholders; now we are extending our information gathering through workshops, at which participants are invited to contribute their own experience of the audit issues.
The workshops take between one and one and a half hours.

We look forward to seeing you on [date, time].

(Project Manager)

At the workshop

The room was prepared in advance, with a copy of the 'map' for each participant, a large version mounted on several sheets of flipchart paper on the wall, and, of course, the coloured Post-it notes. The illustration shows the questions on the map; they aimed to capture 'What Is' as the participants actually experienced it in their own use of knowledge and information in their work, (*see* Figure 3.4 on p71).

When the participants arrived, the project manager welcomed them and explained what would happen. First, they were invited to write their own answers to the map questions on Post-it notes, working individually and anonymously. It was explained that their answers would be posted up on the large map, and that then they would be asked to look at all the contributions, and to discuss any issues arising from the map they had collectively created. The role of the project manager and the audit consultant in the first part of the workshop turned out to be going round unobtrusively, collecting answers as written, and posting them up; as the number grew, it was possible to start grouping them thematically alongside the various questions, to make sub-divisions that reflected common concerns. The process of writing individual answers, we learned from this and other workshops carried out later as the full audit proceeded, took from half to three quarters of an hour. By the end of that time, participants were starting to talk among themselves about the questions, and the map on the wall was surrounded by a lot of vari-coloured Post-its. Time for a tea break, and everybody was ready to gather round the map and discuss what had emerged. The atmosphere was unconstrained, no-body appeared to feel threatened, as they had been able to do their own think-ing individually. A lot of exchanges developed, some revealing very different experi-ence – of access to information, or support from the IT infrastructure – in different parts of the department, others showing common experience running right across. Both those who had recently come to the organization and people with many years of experience made particularly interesting observations – the former comparing it with their previous job, the latter drawing on memories of similar initiatives and what had happened to them.

Discussion typically lasted a further half hour or so, and the proceedings ended with an explanation from the project manager of what would happen next. She would work on the collective map, to put together a coherent and accurate statement of the observations of the participants' experience of the topics; that would lead to a brief interim report, with ideas for any immediate changes that looked as though they could be beneficial and could be implemented without prejudice to the final outcome of the pilot audit. The report would be brought back for discussion with the participants to be finalized before going to the Project Board, and at the same time the department would take delivery of the suggestions for immediate action and decide how to deal with them. Then it was time for the project manager to 'roll up that map' and set about analysing the content in detail. (She created diagrams based on the maps, as an intermediate stage in the analysis, before writing reports. The diagrams used simple graphic coding to identify information flows and such features as: examples of good and bad practice, lack of access to existing information resources, and desired exchanges of information and knowledge.)

This method really comes into its own in workshops, as a combination of individ-ual and group activity, allowing individuals to express their own experience and ideas quickly in their own terms, and without pressure, and making it easy for the group to discuss the results. The essentials are:
● An atmosphere of trust ● A guarantee of anonymity for comments ● A facilitator who is ready to keep in the background.

After using it in a variety of circumstances, with a wide range of people, I have begun to form an idea of why the method works so effectively. I think these are the reasons:
● It's not a 'management consultant's gimmick'. It doesn't ask people to do anything that may make those who aren't of an extravert disposition feel exposed or embar-rassed. ● The first part of the process is done privately and individually – nobody is demanding to see or hear what the people taking part have to say. ● There needn't

4 Information values and culture

4.1 What kinds of K & I does this organization value most? least?

4.2 Does its culture support or discourage exchange of K & I?

4.3 How does it deal with mistakes?

4.4 Barriers that prevent people getting essential information?

3 The organization

3.1 Where is information most critical for your work?

3.2 Most critical issues a) that affect this project b) that it should help resolve?

2 Information environment

2.1 The technology tools you use in handling information?

2.2 The information services you use?

2.3 How effectively do tools and services support your work?

1 Knowledge and information needs

1.1 What do you most need to know about for your work?

1.2 What kinds of information do you need to keep it up to date?

5 Knowledge and information sources

5.1 The most essential information sources you use to keep your knowledge up to date?

5.2 The form they are in? (electronic; print; people)

5.3 How well do they meet your needs? Quality? Ease of finding what you need in them?

5.4 How do you locate new information sources?

6 Information processes and products

6.1 Who manages information in your department? Their training?

6.2 Does performance appraisal cover information use?

6.3 How effective is information exchange: between departments? within departments?

6.4 Who provides you with the information you need for work? How helpful is it?

6.5 What kinds of information do you provide as part of your work? To outside? Inside? Form?

7 Reflections

7.1 Changes that would help you to make more effective use of K & I?

▲
Information and knowledge mapping

Figure 3.4
Information audit map for collecting the experience
of staff from different departments of the organization

be anything to identify individuals ● The framework of the map and the questions provides a visible structure that helps people transfer ideas from inside their heads to the outside world without the usual problems of written composition – the limited writing space available on the Post-its helps ● By bringing many ideas into the same plane, it allows them to be 'read' in the way that diagrams are read, and to see relationships among them more quickly than is possible with written descriptions. In effect, it enables the group to enter territory that is normally inhabited only by designers ● It allows collective creation without individual exposure, and the end product can be viewed and commented on collectively without attribution of specific responses ● It's low-tech and direct, and can be completed before concentration lapses.

Reading list

CHECKLAND, P. and SCHOLES, J. (2001), *Soft Systems Methodology in Action*, Chichester: John Wiley & Sons. If you want to consider using soft systems methodology in information auditing, this is an authoritative introduction, and a good read into the bargain, with lots of the clear hand-drawn diagrams that are characteristic of the method. Checkland and his collaborators created soft systems methodology more than 30 years ago, as a tool for understanding how organizations work. This volume reprints the key text first published in 1990 with a new introductory chapter that looks back over the history of the ideas, and offers a summing up of the process from today's point of view.

HENCZEL, S. (2001A), *The Information Audit. A Practical Guide*, Munich: K G Saur. Lives up to its name, and tells you exactly how to do things. Good practical advice on using analysis tools.

... (2001B), 'The information audit as a first step towards effective knowledge management', *Information Outlook*, June, 48–62. From information audit, to knowledge audit, to knowledge management strategy.

ORNA, E. (2000), 'The human face of information auditing', *Managing Information*, 7 (4) 40–42. 'Organizations consist of human beings who don't leave their feelings ... or their eccentricities and cussedness, on the doorstep when they enter their place of work. To insist on assuming that organizations are wholly rational entities is really flying in the face of common sense ...' Suggestions from experience for dealing with organizational culture.

Information auditing: interpreting and presenting the findings 4.1

Facts do not 'speak for themselves'; they are read in the light of meaning.
–STEPHEN J. GOULD. (1991)

Introduction

The last chapter took us as far as the process of finding out. Now we move on to making sense of the findings, telling the organization about what they mean, and recommending action. Of course this is not a straight linear progression; within the broad movement forward, there are doublings back and anticipations of what comes next, and people who have been closely involved in the process will inevitably find they are extracting possible meanings from what they find as they go on. This can be put to good use; supplementary questions can be asked to test the validity of interim interpretations. But final judgements need to be suspended until the full picture is available from whatever the audit has undertaken to look at.

Step 6: (see Figure 3.1, p49)
Interpreting the findings – matching what is with what should be

We return now to the steps in the audit process. Interpretation of the audit findings is as important as the findings themselves, and the quality of the interpretation is critical for the success of the action that follows from the audit.

Matching what is with what should be

As explained earlier (*see* pp46–49) the heart of information auditing is matching what the organization's goals imply it should be doing with information, and what the audit has shown it is doing. The focus for interpretation is the points where the two differ and those where they match, because these are the most significant for the contribution information makes to achieving organizational objectives.

Burk and Horton (1988) provide a useful means of identifying these significant points, as shown in Figure 4.1 (*see* p74).

Two examples will help to make the point clear:

1 A situation where information is of high strategic importance, but there is a mismatch between how it is being used and the key objectives.

A CHAMBER OF COMMERCE
Main goal: To retain existing members, and recruit new ones, by providing relevant products/services.

Strategic importance of information to achieving this goal: **High.**
What should be:
* High quality-information about members and potential members   * Easy access to information about their business interests.

What is:

• Elderly membership database • Allows only for limited information about members • Needs special reports to extract information about their business • Staff responsible for database haven't time/don't understand why colleagues want it.

Interpretation: High strategic importance of information is undermined by:

• Lack of access to essential information • Poor IT support • Failures of understanding and communication.

Score for this aspect of information use: **Minus score;** a threat to the organization's future if it continues.

2 A situation where the high strategic importance of information to achieving a key objective is well matched by how the organization is using information.

A FIRM MANUFACTURING QUALITY SPORTS CLOTHING

Main goal: To maintain competitive position by developing new products, matching customers' needs.

Strategic importance of information to achieving this goal: **High.**

What should be:

• High-quality information about customer response to products, lifestyle, preferences • Flowing well between customers and the business.

What is:

• Good relations and information flow between: ○ Customer care staff and customers ○ Sales staff and customers ○ Customer care, sales, marketing and R&D • Sophisticated customer database.

Interpretation: High strategic importance of information is supported by:

• The kind of information collected • The ways in which people use it and interact with information and with each other • IT and systems.

Score for this aspect of information use: **High;** there are potential lessons here for other areas of the business.

When it comes to interpreting the range of findings in a way that gives a sense of the whole picture, there are various possibilities. The Australian Securities Commission (referred to in Chapter 2 of this book) used the well-tried SWOT analysis (Strengths, Weaknesses, Opportunities, Threats) very effectively in presenting its information audit findings. Booth and Haines (1993) provide an interesting example of using the 'holistic' soft systems methodology in an information audit to define the current information system as perceived by staff of the organization. A 'rich picture' of the systems and groups of people making up the organization and its environment, created from information gathered during interviews and discussions, was used to devise 'root definitions' of:

• **C**lients or customers of the systems
• '**A**ctors' responsible for the main activities
• **T**ransformation processes by which inputs are modified and outputs produced
• '**W**orld view' – that is, the 'philosophy' informing the systems
• **O**wnership of the system – who has the controlling power
• **E**nvironment in which the system operates.

(The initials make up the acronym CATWOE which is often used as a shorthand expression for this aspect of the soft systems approach.)

Relating audit findings to organizational objectives

		Good news	Bad news
1 What objective does this information resource/activity contribute to?			
2 Strategic importance of the objective to organization's success?		High	High
3 Strategic importance of this information resource/activity to the objective?		High	High
4 How effectively does it contribute?		Well	Poorly

Figure 4.1
Questions to help in relating audit findings to the organization's objectives (based on Burk and Horton, 1988)

The picture and the definitions were used in interpreting the audit findings.[1]

Another approach to interpreting the whole picture takes up the initial analysis of what the organization needs to know to achieve its goals, the information it needs to support that knowledge, and the information interactions it requires in order to act on the knowledge (*see* Tables 2.1, p21; 2.2, pp22–24; and 2.3 pp27–32). This means using the 'what should be' statement directly as a framework for presenting the findings about 'what is', so that each statement of the desirable state of affairs is immediately followed by the actual situation. Table 4.1 shows an example based on an analysis similar to that of Tables 2.1–2.3, for a company.

Directly relating the actual and the desirable makes it possible to move on to visualizing where they converge and diverge; Figure 4.2 shows an example (*see* pp77–78). A graphic representation makes a good starting point for planning the report on the audit, which is the next topic for consideration.

1 I recently enjoyed the experience of helping to run a practical course which combined information auditing with the soft systems approach. Besides generating a lot of hilarity, the experience of creating a rich picture and root definition for their own organizations illuminated them from a new direction for participants, who were then able to use the insights constructively in planning an information audit.

Knowledge and know-how	Information required to maintain knowledge requirements	
Content	**'Containers'**	
• About customers	Who and where they are Products bought Transactions Retention rates/losses	Database, allowing access via multiple features

Findings:
Database acknowledged to be unsatisfactory for access to information now required; intensive efforts and investment being made to upgrade system

	Views of value and quality Level of satisfaction with products/services New requirements	Reports from people in regular contact with them Reports on research

Findings:
Effort has recently been put into developing feedback, including training for staff in this area, but information needs and interactions are not yet clearly defined.

Research commissioned in the past hasn't always been satisfactory; briefs sometimes not clear; where findings have been relevant, often not acted on.

Awareness on the part of managers now improving; research strategy under development

• About economic and social context in which the company works	Demographic trends Age structure of population Economic situation Employment patterns Lifestyle/social trends	Appropriate statistical series Periodicals and press Research reports On-line external databases Internet
• About competition and innovation in the industry	Situation of competing companies Their products and services	Periodicals and press 'Intelligence' reports compiled from various sources

Findings:
Press and PR section within External Relations provides cuttings service; some periodical subscriptions; access to one on-line business database, but used by few people.

Awareness among some senior managers that much more external information of significance to the business is needed, and that there is a big information gap here.

No manager with specific responsibility for developing information resources of this kind, and no staff with relevant professional qualifications

Table 4.1
The information which a company needs:
what should be and what is

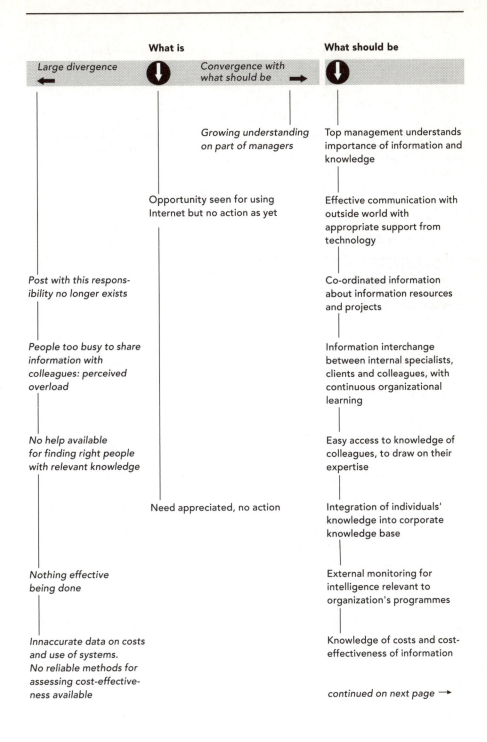

What is   **What should be**

Large divergence ←   *Convergence with what should be* →

Growing understanding on part of managers   Top management understands importance of information and knowledge

Opportunity seen for using Internet but no action as yet   Effective communication with outside world with appropriate support from technology

Post with this respons-ibility no longer exists   Co-ordinated information about information resources and projects

People too busy to share information with colleagues: perceived overload   Information interchange between internal specialists, clients and colleagues, with continuous organizational learning

No help available for finding right people with relevant knowledge   Easy access to knowledge of colleagues, to draw on their expertise

Need appreciated, no action   Integration of individuals' knowledge into corporate knowledge base

Nothing effective being done   External monitoring for intelligence relevant to organization's programmes

Innaccurate data on costs and use of systems. No reliable methods for assessing cost-effective-ness available   Knowledge of costs and cost-effectiveness of information

continued on next page →

Figure 4.2
What should be and what is – convergence and divergence

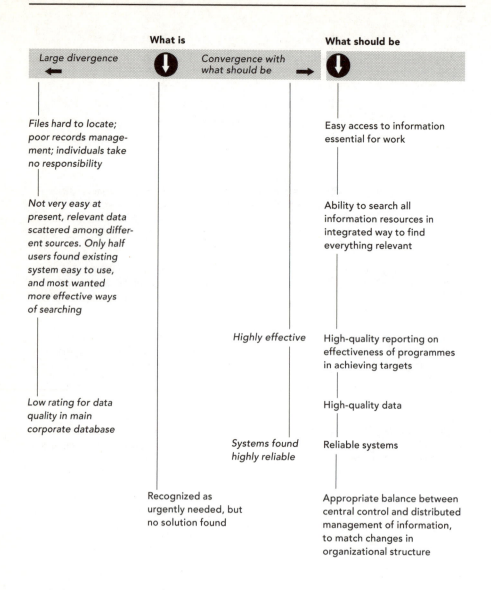

What is

Large divergence ← Convergence with what should be →

What should be

Files hard to locate; poor records management; individuals take no responsibility

Easy access to information essential for work

Not very easy at present, relevant data scattered among different sources. Only half users found existing system easy to use, and most wanted more effective ways of searching

Ability to search all information resources in integrated way to find everything relevant

Highly effective

High-quality reporting on effectiveness of programmes in achieving targets

Low rating for data quality in main corporate database

High-quality data

Systems found highly reliable

Reliable systems

Recognized as urgently needed, but no solution found

Appropriate balance between central control and distributed management of information, to match changes in organizational structure

Figure 4.2
What should be and what is – convergence and divergence

Step 7: (see Figure 3.1, p49)
Presenting the audit findings – a selling job

If we do not pay heed to how we make the knowledge acquired in the course of the audit visible and manageable for others who have not shared in the process, we run the risk of burying it under a heap of words and wearying the reader into exasperation or misunderstanding of the essential message. And in that case, we shall have great difficulty in selling the product, which is what we must do if the organization is to get a useful return on the effort invested in the audit.

Reporting on the audit

The report is all too often the stage at which value, instead of being added, is subtracted. The main dangers are:
● Too much prose: prose is good for developing arguments and telling stories; but it acts to obscure relationships of numerical information, and it is often unhelpful when we need to draw attention to particular points or to summarize conclusions ● Too much detail: it is easy to forget that material through which we can find our way with easy familiarity is likely to be an impenetrable thicket for all but those who are involved in that particular aspect of the organization's work ● Not enough signposts: readers need to know where they are going, where they are at present, and where they have already been. Most reports give them little help in the way of an informative contents list, carefully structured heading hierarchy, and cross-reference ● Not enough stopping points: readers need the chance to pause at the end of each step in the argument, and to review where it has brought them ● Not enough aids to verification: it is a courtesy to readers to refer them to the places where they will find the evidence that supports particular arguments ● Discourtesy, or downright insult, to the eye: badly reproduced reports, lines far too long for comfortable reading, inappropriate typefaces, ill-prepared graphics, and tables that make it hard to identify and compare critical data – all these are still too common, and readers who meet them are likely to be consciously or unconsciously influenced against the content.
   Reports should:
● Not demand too much reading time (an executive summary at the beginning is a good investment; willingness to read is generally inversely related to how exalted the reader is in the organization) ● Express the findings in the language which the people to whom it is addressed use and are accustomed to (they will not learn information-specialist speak, so it is the obligation of authors to translate anything esoteric into their terms) ● Emphasize: opportunities for using information to bring benefits to the organization's most important goals; and threats and risks that need immediate action ● Give examples of: good use of information that adds value; poor use that causes loss of value; beneficial changes ('quick wins') which have already been made during the audit as a result of what has come to light (the Australian Securities and Investments Commission case study, Orna 1999, p197, is a good example) ● Present proposals for: short-term low-risk changes that can bring 'quick wins'; the next stages of auditing (if the audit is being done by stages); longer-term changes and phases towards them.

And finally, they should take every opportunity to sell thinking as a low-risk and highly cost-effective activity (for an example of a successful national institution which believes this and acts on it, see the British Library case study, Orna, 1999, p213). Decisions on structure, format, layout etc are best taken by the writers of the report, in the light of their knowledge of the organization and of the people they are addressing, and drawing on whatever professional expertise is available to them. (For examples of approaches to reporting on audits, *see* the case studies of the Australian Securities and Investments Commission, the University of North London, and Surrey Police in Orna, 1999.)

Communication

Presenting the audit findings and recommendations for action on them is a critical point in the process because it determines whether the audit will be acted on, or added to the tally of dead and unceremoniously buried initiatives. The process of face-to-face presentation is a combination of communicating information and selling a course of action. The people who have managed the audit should take the lead in presentation and in arguing for their recommendations; and the findings should be presented to those who have participated, as well as to the top management team, in fulfilment of the undertaking to give them the opportunity of discussing the findings and contributing to decisions on action.

The assets which the presenters can draw on are the knowledge gained from the audit, which is their unique property until it is presented, the authority which comes from knowledge, and the relationship they have built up with the 'management champion' and with colleagues throughout the organization during the audit.

Preparation

Because presentation to the top management team is such a critical stage, it is essential to devote adequate time to preparing and trying it out. If there has been a steering committee, they are the ideal audience for a 'dress rehearsal'. Otherwise the critical observer for the trial run will have to be the 'management champion'. Whoever fulfils the role, their job is to pick up things that are likely to be misunderstood, to give rise to questions or to hostile responses, or to be seen as threats to power structures – and to suggest alternative approaches, different ways of putting the same point, how to deal with opposition, and what arguments to address to potential allies and to likely opponents. It is particularly important to discuss possible structural changes implicit in the findings and recommendations and their 'political implications', and to develop strategies for presenting them. Fortunately, the experience gained during the audit process is likely to have deepened the audit team's insight into power structures and prevalent 'world views'.

As with a written report, so too with presentation it is good sense to choose presentation techniques that are familiar to and approved of by the people addressed. It is equally important to make sure you know how to use them really well, and that they work on the crucial occasion. Readers will certainly have experienced manifestations of the rule that computer-based demonstrations which work perfectly in rehearsal fall over on the night. (This sort of thing actually happened long before computers were invented; my father used to tell me about the advice he was offered as a pupil teacher 80 years ago by his science master, when learning how to demonstrate the principles of distillation to a class – 'Put a spoonful of brandy in the collecting vessel before you start.')

Presentation outwards into the organization, as well as upwards to top management, should, as recommended earlier (*see* pp50–52), be provided for in planning the audit. It is of equal importance to the 'upstream' presentation, and demands a different approach, with no less rigorous preparation. The aim is not only to inform and to sell ideas for action; it is critical to use this occasion as a forum for interaction and exchange of views on an equal basis, where people who have contributed information to the audit are able to consider what use has been made of it, to see how their contribution matches other inputs, correct inaccurate representations, discuss the conclusions drawn and recommendations made, and propose alternative or additional courses of action. This outward presentation is an opportunity for spreading knowledge of the audit process through the organization, and for identifying and drawing in new people to work on the next stages.

Making the presentation can be a challenging experience; but those who undertake it should remember the advantage they have acquired by becoming the people who are most knowledgeable about what the organization does with information. That gives them the authority to be heard when they propose action based on what they have learned, and it lends merited value to their judgements. So, if it comes your way to present the results of an information audit, remember:

● Your audience will take you at the value you set upon yourself ● Use the authority of honestly gained knowledge ● Make sure they see the view you want them to see – it is part of the role entrusted to you to be a reliable guide.

Steps 8–10: (see Figure 3.1, p49)
Following up the audit

At this point the first round of information auditing is completed, but, rather than an end, it marks the beginning of new activities – covered in later chapters – as well as another cycle of the auditing process.

The presentation of audit results should flow without interruption into decisions, and decisions into action. The outcome of presentation should be an action plan, which should aim for:

● Essential changes to avoid any immediate threats ● Quick benefits in key areas, to keep up the momentum and maintain commitment to change ● Maintaining the communications links established in the audit. ● A definitive statement of the organization's information policy (*see* Chapter 5, pp93–96) ● A start on developing an organizational information strategy to ensure that the business strategy benefits from an 'organizational knowledge base' which is kept constantly up to date ● Establishing appropriate criteria for monitoring and evaluating changes as they are implemented ● Making the information audit into a regular monitoring and evaluation exercise ● Regular reporting on information developments at the top level as a feed into business strategy development ● Starting to assess the cost-effectiveness of information use and its contribution to the value of the organization's assets.

Summary

- The heart of information auditing is matching 'what is' with 'what should be'
- The focus for interpreting the findings from an audit is the points where:
1 Information is of high strategic importance for the organization and there is a big difference between the reality and what should be
2 Information is of high strategic importance for the organization and there is a good match.
- Presenting audit findings is a selling job, and deserves full attention and intensive preparation, so that the decision makers understand the message and buy it, and the organization gets a useful return on the effort put into auditing • Presentation outwards into the organization is as important as presentation upwards to top management • In both face-to-face and written presentation, probably the most important factor in selling the ideas is to express them in the language which the audience uses • And the most important idea to sell is: Thinking is a low-risk and highly cost-effective activity!

References

BOOTH, A. and HAINES, M. (1993), 'Information audit: whose line is it anyway?', *Health Libraries Review*, 10 (4), 224–232.

BURK, C. F. Jr and HORTON, F. W. Jr (1988), *Infomap: a complete guide to discovering corporate information resources*, Englewood Cliffs, NJ: Prentice Hall.

GOULD, S. J. (1991). 'The validation of continental drift' in *Ever since Darwin*, London: Penguin Books.

ORNA, E. (1999), *Practical Information Policies*, Ed2, Aldershot: Gower.

To begin with, one cautionary tale. This is the story of a report that undid a lot of the good from the actual audit.

A cautionary tale

The occasion was an information consultancy assignment which had gone well; good relations had been established with the client organization, and its staff had provided excellent information to the consultants. But when it came to the report and recommendations, the first version caused trouble. It was expressed in terms unfamiliar to the senior managers it was addressed to, who lacked IT experience and were innocent of any acquaintance with information jargon. The headings differed from those used in the course of the assignment; the evidence on which the recommendations were based was not clearly stated; structure and sequence were difficult to follow, and the visual presentation obscured rather than clarified. In fact it exemplified many of the features which can subtract value as listed on p79. The report roused anxiety because it was so difficult to understand and so different from what the client had expected. Though an amended final version was accepted, enough trust was lost to result in rejection of some key recommendations for action, disappointment to staff who had hoped for much-needed changes, and no further contact between the business and the consultants.

A different approach

The organization whose information audit we looked at in the previous chapter approached this stage of the proceedings in a rather different way. We left the story at the point when key stakeholder interviews and workshops had been held for the pilot audit.

Reporting on the pilot audit

Because all the interviews and the workshops had collected information under a standard set of headings, the material was roughly categorized to start with. There was still a lot of work to be done in sub-dividing it further, bringing related responses together, and identifying similarities and differences in the experiences reported, but the main structure of the report was there. The project manager applied her knowledge of the organization to this task. In the course of it, she identified small beneficial changes that could readily be made without waiting for the end of the audit. She and the consultant looked for particularly significant issues, which suggested either a damaging gap between 'What is' and 'What should be', or instances of good practice that exemplified what should be happening.

The draft report on the pilot audit that resulted was, as promised, taken back to representatives of the department involved for discussion and feedback. The department took over the ideas for minor changes which had emerged, to consider how they could be implemented, and the project manager amended the report for presentation to the Project Board. It's worth quoting two items from the report: the 'What should be/What is' table, and the areas recommended for investigation in the next stages of the audit.

What should be	What is
Staff	
1	**1**
Interact with customers	Interactions take place without full knowl-
Gain knowledge about them	edge of all contacts between the organization
Provide K&I to support them	and its customers; in consequence,
Bring K from interactions into the	K&I support for them is less effective than
organization; exchange with other	it should be
stakeholders; input K into organization's	Knowledge derived from interactions is either
information store	not put into information store, or is input in a
	form that make it less accessible/ less useful
	than it should be.
	Inadequate support for this process; input
	to a variety of stores; no single way in to
	all relevant information
2	**2**
Maintain core knowledge about:	No single point of access to all essential
Customers, suppliers, external partners,	information held internally in the organ-
organizations, businesses	ization; poor support for locating good
Specialist topics/disciplines	quality external sources and keeping track
Own activities and results, contacts, inter-	of new ones, so people rely on a small
actions, I&K resources, etc	number of sources and risk missing essential
	information
	No standard procedures for documenting
	projects and results
3	**3**
Maintain context knowledge about:	No clear processes for helping maintain exter-
Legislation	nal or internal context knowledge Products by
Government policies	which this kind of information
Economic/social context	is delivered don't help
The organization's policies/strategies;	No single authoritative source for policies
other departments	Information about activities of other depart-
	ments and teams within own department
	hard to come by
4	**4**
Contribute to/influence:	So is information about relevant projects to
The organization's policies/strategies	which staff might contribute, or which they
Projects of other departments	might influence

What should be	What is
5 Make outcomes and lessons of projects and initiatives accessible to stakeholders by inputting to information store	**5** No consistent procedures for recording lessons, particularly of things that went wrong; perception in some areas that such things are buried, or subject to 'blame culture'
6 Manage information resources for which they have responsibility	**6** No provision to help people who have to manage information resources as part of their job, but without any training
7 Know who are the stakeholders in the results of their work; know who is doing similar work; exchange information with them, within and between departments	**7** No provision for maintaining this kind of information; lack of it is seen as a hindrance to effective working

Management

What should be	What is
8 Has a clear policy and strategy for the use of K&I, based on its key business objectives, and supporting its business processes	**8** No policy/strategy exists
9 Defines the K&I content it needs for its business, the principles to be followed in using K&I, and the obligations and rights of staff in this matter	**9** No definition of required content No statements of principles, etc Perception by staff that kinds of K&I that they find from experience are essential for their work are those least valued by management
10 Ensures that each part of the organization identifies the K&I it requires to achieve its part in the organization's objectives	**10** No action in this respect as yet
11 Keeps staff fully informed of external developments critical for the organization's work, of the developments in the organization's own policies and strategies, and changes affecting its work	**11** Staff report problems in this respect; variable quality of 'cascading' No single authoritative up-to-date source
12 Follows consistent processes for downward and upward flow of information in the organization Responds to information which it has requested and provides feedback	**12** Staff report lack of consistency in downward flow; lack of response and feedback to information provided at management request

continued on next page

What should be	What is
13 Provides resources for applying professional knowledge and skills in knowledge and information management, and in relevant technologies, so as to develop and maintain the services, systems, tools, processes and products that are essential to support all staff in finding, using and exchanging I&K	**13** One resource – the library – has been removed No provision for central professional co-ordination of KM&IM Staff report problems, and anxiety about risks and losses from having to cope with information tasks outside their professional competence The organization loses from staff not being able to devote the maximum proportion of working time to exercising the skills and knowledge they are employed to contribute
14 Encourages and supports the exchange of I&K and good information management, through performance appraisal, and through training policy	**14** Rarely covered in performance appraisal; no consistent practice Training policy does not specifically address this area; line managers are not supported in their responsibilities for it. Training policy does not specifically address this area; line managers are not supported in their responsibilities for it

Areas for investigation in next stages of audit

In the light of this pilot information audit we can indicate four key areas for action which will be tested in the next stages of the organization-wide audit; if found valid, they will form the subject of our final recommendations.

1 Organization
● A practical knowledge and information policy, with clear objectives for using knowledge and information to support business objectives ● Flexible organizational structure related to how information and knowledge need to flow, to promote exchanges across boundaries ● Single vision of how the organization should market and present itself to its customers, to guide how information is presented to the outside world.

2 Unified 'information repository'
● Kinds of knowledge and information across the organization that are critical for its success ● Essential interactions and flows of knowledge and information across organizational boundaries and between the organization and its 'outside world'
● Co-ordinated, fully indexed repository of essential existing, and new, knowledge and information resources, accessed via single interface, that all staff can draw on and contribute to.

3 Support for strategic use of knowledge and information
● Professional management of information repository through a team drawing on appropriate existing specialisms within the organization (knowledge and informa-

tion management, systems/IT, human resources, communications); responsible for co-ordinating, developing, managing information repository; implementing and developing policy in this area ● Support for all staff in information-management aspects of their work, through training, including improved and individualized induction process ● Procedures for capturing results and disseminating lessons of experience – including those from mistakes.

4 Infrastructure/tools
● Integrated, 'interoperable' IT systems to support development and use of information repository ● Development of the intranet as key element in access to information.

Other activities
During the next stages of the information audit we will:
● Benchmark – in order to make comparisons and learn from other organizations who have used information auditing as a step towards knowledge management
● Link in with the change-management unit and other relevant initiatives.

The Project Board accepted the report, and agreed to extend the audit to all departments, using the same questions and topics, and the methods that had been tested in the pilot.

Final report

The audit was duly completed; thanks to the experience gained in the pilot, the process became easier and quicker with each round. The framework established in the pilot made it simple to fit new information into the appropriate places as gathered, and to spot similarities and exceptions as they came up. This meant that creating the final report to the Project Board, which would form the basis of a short paper for the organization's executive board, was an easier task, done more quickly than the report on the pilot.

The report contents list is given below, because, while specific to the particular organization, it makes a good model for coverage, structure and sequence. Useful presentation features in the report included diagrams; tables; icons for related projects; boxes bringing out examples of good practice and initiatives; brief case studies from other audits to make specific points, and a telling example showing the estimated loss to the organization, in terms of time wasted and salary costs, created by unsuccessful searches for information. (For other examples of such costs, *see* Parnell, 2001.)

Executive Summary

Introduction
Background and methodology
Current relevance

Key findings
Knowledge and information needs for meeting objectives

– Shortcomings in meeting them
Information sources used to keep knowledge up to date
– Shortcomings in information sources

Information environment – support for getting and using information
– Professional support
– Training and performance appraisal
– Tools and technology
– Shortcomings in information environment

Information processes and products
– Inputting knowledge from people's minds into information resources
– Finding information sources, and locating essential information in them
– Information exchanges, communication
– Information products
– Shortcomings in information processes and products

What the organization's business objectives mean in terms of knowledge and information
– Shortcomings in this respect

How the organization's culture and structure affect the use of knowledge and information
– Shortcomings in this respect

Immediate action recommended and already initiated
Designated responsibility for information within teams, and support and training for those responsible

Paper file management processes review

Model of how all key strategies, high-level objectives and business targets fit together

Brief explanations of what all parts of the organization are doing, and a 'who does what' guide

Review of internal communications to improve information exchange, sharing and dissemination within the organization

Taxonomy workshop as start for meeting requirements for indexing and information structuring

Study of how to share file stores across sites

Lessons learnt during the audit process

Recommendations

Proposed next steps
Evaluation of the process of information auditing, recommendations for future applications

Executive Summary – a positive start

The first item in the final report is the Executive Summary – it takes that place, because its job is to draw attention to the messages in the accompanying report that the authors want to make sure the readers – who may have only a slight acquaintance with what's been going on – take on board. It is a good idea to give them something encouraging to read near the start – whatever 'strengths or assets' have been found in the audit – before pointing to the shortcomings that undermine the strengths. The summary must give clear references at every point to the relevant sections of the full report, as in this quotation about the recommendations:

Recommendations

The top-level recommendations summarized below cover key areas where action is essential in order to overcome the knowledge and information deficiencies, and to capitalize on opportunities revealed by the audit.

⚬ That the Board publish their commitment to the principle that information is a corporate asset to be shared, and encourage all departments to put this principle into practice ⚬ The immediate action required is that the Board should endorse the principles recommended, and should make appropriate people within the organization responsible for implementing in practice the actions recommended in the report [*see* p90].

Recommendations – not too many!

Showering top management with dozens of detailed recommendations is a surefire recipe for, at best, delay in response, and at worst rejection. The 'recommendations' section of the final report was deliberately restricted to a small number of 'in-principle' recommendations that gave the 'Top Of The Organization' (usually referred to by the acronym TOTO) proposals that were appropriate for top-level decision, leaving detailed interpretation and implementation where it rightly belongs, with staff who have appropriate knowledge and expertise – in this instance, the audit team and the colleagues from different departments who had worked with them on the audit. Each recommendation was followed by:

⚬ Reason for recommending this (with a pointer to where the report gave the relevant evidence) ● How implementation will contribute to meeting audit objectives and contribute to the organization's business processes ● Consequences (including costs and risks) of not implementing ● Responsibility for implementing ● Resources required ● Timescale for implementation.

Recommendations

The four top-level recommendations below cover key areas where action is essential in order to overcome the knowledge and information deficiencies, and to capitalize on opportunities revealed by the audit.

The immediate action required is that the board should endorse the principles recommended, and should make appropriate people within the organization responsible for implementation in practice.

Area 1: The organization's policy for knowledge and information

Recommendation 1
That the organization adopts and promotes a practical knowledge and information policy, which:
● Sets clear objectives for using knowledge and information to support business objectives and business processes ● Defines the knowledge and information content essential for its work ● States organizational principles for using knowledge and information, and the obligations and rights of the organization and its staff in this matter.

Reason for recommendation
● It is essential to demonstrate management commitment to and understanding of knowledge and information management; without it, there will be no guarantee that the findings of the audit are taken seriously, or that action will be taken to overcome the shortcomings revealed ● The audit findings show that staff are not clear about how they should use knowledge and information in meeting corporate objectives
● They also suggest that staff perceive that top management sets a low value on the kinds of knowledge and information which they themselves find essential for their work. Whether or not this is actually the case, the fact that such a disparity is perceived presents dangers for the organization. A policy of this kind would help bridge it, and would make an essential point of reference for necessary changes.

Area 2: Unifying the organization's 'information repository'

Recommendation 2
That the organization continues to develop, by appropriate stages, co-ordinated knowledge and information repositories that eventually all staff can both draw on and contribute to. The long-term objective is to give easy and effective access through a single interface to the complete range of fully indexed internal resources, and to relevant external resources.

Reason for recommendation
● The audit has shown clearly the kind of knowledge and information that are essential, and equally clearly the lack of coherence between existing resources,

the absence of certain essential resources, and the incompleteness, poor quality or inaccessibility of others ● The effects of this situation: existing information resources are not properly exploited; critical needs are not met; resources are not kept up to date, and are not used because their quality is suspect; valuable staff time is lost on unproductive searches for information; risks are incurred and opportunities missed because of lack of full access to essential information.

Area 3: Support for strategic use of knowledge and information

Recommendation 3
That the organization build on its existing strengths in knowledge management and on initiatives already taken by the KM team, to develop integrated know-ledge and information management by a group drawing on appropriate existing specialisms within the organization (including knowledge and information man-agement, systems /IT, HR, communications), headed by a manager at an appropriate level.

Responsibilities of the group: developing, co-ordinating, and managing the unified knowledge and information repository; developing and implementing policy in this area; contributing to the development of the organization's business strategies; supporting staff who manage specific information resources.

Reason for recommendation
● The role and responsibilities of the KM team appear as yet not to be well under-stood within the organization ● Although today it is accepted by leaders in good practice in KM that the knowledge which individuals need to use in their work cannot be maintained and managed successfully without the support of properly managed resources of information, this level of information management is not provided for in the organization. The KM team themselves are well aware of this and wish to remedy the deficiency (For definitions of the complementary roles of KM and IM, see Annex A) ● The organization employs high-quality information professionals, but they currently do not have the opportunity of exercising their professional skills to its full advantage. Lack of support in managing information is a key cause for the kind of problems reported by every department and every individual contributing to the audit ● This recommendation is the essential com-plement to Recommendation 2.

Area 4: Infrastructure/IT tools

Recommendation 4
That the organization tests and thinks about providing the appropriate IT systems to support the development and use of a single corporate knowledge and informa-tion repository. In the meantime the development of the organization's intranet should be seen as the key element in access to information.

Reason for recommendation
● The audit has shown clearly that the use of appropriate tools and technology is important for capturing, storing and managing knowledge and information ● There is a fragmented awareness and inconsistent use of IT tools, which equates to fragmented and inconsistent capture, storage and management of knowledge and information, so creating barriers to the exchange and flow of information

• The intranet and website are considered not very effective as 'meta-information products' which contain a range of information products. A lack of structure, of aids to finding information, and of indexing makes them difficult to use.

A coda about language in reports

On p79 I recommend expressing findings in the language which the people to whom reports are addressed use and are accustomed to (as against using the specialized jargon of the information management or IT community). But what do you do if the organization itself habitually uses its own impenetrable bureaucratic jargon in its internal communications? The organization where the audit described in these pages was carried out was more than a little prone to strange terminology, abbreviations and acronyms, and tortured syntax that effectively obscured sense. Even those who felt they had to use it when they wrote documents acknowledged that they didn't much enjoy either writing them, or reading the results. The audit team decided A) that they couldn't bear to use it and B) that they would make straightforward words and syntax such as human beings use in ordinary life a selling point for the audit – something that would distinguish it from the usual run of organizational documents and by that novelty gain proper attention. The response justified their decision.

Reference
PARNELL, N. (2001), 'Managing information overload', *Business Information Review*, 18 (1) 45–50.

From information audit to information policy

Managers from different functions might join together to form a permanent network or team, formulating policies and processes to assist in specifically managing information behavior.

The policies and processes could include determining information steward-ship in each department; clarification of when information sharing and hoarding are appropriate; the specific behaviors called for when the company commits to managing by fact (rather than rumor or intuition); and recommended processes, such as defining information architecture and strategy in behaviorally sensitive ways, for information professionals. The rules for such crucial information issues deserve a formal place in corporate procedure manuals ...'

–DAVENPORT, THOMAS H. (1997), p105

Introduction

In Chapter 2 (p19) I argued for the positive gains that come from starting with an understanding of the organization: 'what it seeks to achieve, where it is trying to go, how it sets about its business, and how it sees itself and its outside world'. Among those gains were:

> ● A picture of 'what should be' – if this is what the organization is trying to do, with this structure and this culture, then this is what it ought to be trying to do with information and knowledge ● Some first ideas about how that could be expressed in a policy for information.

The last two chapters have been devoted to the business of finding out what the organization is actually doing with information and knowledge and matching it against the 'what should be' picture, so as to make well-founded decisions about action to capitalize on good matches and improve bad ones. We agreed, I hope, that it was important not to lose the impetus, and for decisions to flow without interruption into actions. One of the first and most significant actions should be to refine whatever ideas about information policy we developed initially, in the light of what we now know, and to make that policy a firmly stated part of the organiza-tion's guiding principles.

Refining the information policy

We defined organizational information policy (*see* p8) as:

> A policy founded on an organization's overall objectives, and the priorities within them, which defines, at a general level:
> ● The objectives of information use in the organization, and the priorities among them ● What 'information' means in the context of what the organization is in

business for ● The principles on which it will manage information ● Principles for the use of human resources in managing information ● Principles for the use of technology to support information management ● The principles it will apply in relation to establishing the cost-effectiveness of information and knowledge.

Let us now look in more detail at what a policy should cover and how it might be expressed.

What an information policy should cover

What follows is an example of what an information policy could cover. It is based in part on actual policies developed in various organizations, and in part on experience and reflections over the past eight years. It is not offered as a model for copying, rather as a source of ideas about what might be appropriate for specific organizations. I doubt if any organization would wish to take the whole lot on board at one go; most, I guess, will be happier to start with a few basic principles which they see as particularly relevant to their own situation, and there's nothing wrong with that. An information policy can, and should, be revisited from time to time, and further refined in the light of experience. What *is* important is that the policy should be expressed in terms that match the organization's goals and character (*see* 'Nailing down the basic principles' below, p96), and that it should be used throughout the organization as a focus for thinking about how it uses knowledge and information.

Name of organization
Policy for the use of information and knowledge

Basic obligations

1 Information resources are the property of the organization as a whole, not of individuals or groups within it.
2 It is part of the job of everyone in the organization to:
● Be aware of what they need to know to do their job, and of the information needs of the people with whom they interact in their work ● Use information in order to keep their knowledge in an appropriate state to support their work
● Interchange information and knowledge with colleagues and with people outside the organization to help it achieve its aims ● Manage conscientiously any resources of information for which they are responsible.
3 It is the organization's obligation to provide education, training and support to enable them to do so.
4 The organization will respect knowledge in the minds of people as their own permanent property; in return, they will use it to support their work and that of their colleagues, and make it available to the organization's knowledge base on leaving the organization.

The policy

We will:
1 Define what knowledge we need to achieve our goals, the information we need

Information strategy in practice

to maintain the knowledge, and the ways in which people in the organization need to use knowledge and information.

2 Keep the definitions up to date as our goals evolve and change.

3 Audit our use of information and knowledge regularly to ensure that we have what we need and are using it appropriately and to good effect.

4 Ensure that appropriate information is acquired from outside, and generated inside, to allow us to do what we need to do with information knowledge.

5 Exploit it fully, to meet all current needs, and to help us develop to meet changes in our goals and in the environment in which we operate.

6 Ensure that it reaches, on time, and in the right format, all the people who need to use it.

7 Identify the people responsible for managing specific resources of information, and those who are 'stakeholders' in them, and ensure that the authority of the managers of information resources matches the responsibility they carry.

8 Provide for a co-ordinated overview of our total resources of knowledge and information.

9 Promote information interchange between managers of information resources, and between them and stakeholders.

10 Develop and maintain an infrastructure of systems and information technology to support the management of information resources and information interac tions with the organization and between it and the outside world.

11 Use knowledge and information ethically in all our internal and external deaings, so as to preserve and enhance our reputation.[1]

12 Pursue maximum openness of access to information inside the organization and for our 'outside world'.

13 Safeguard our resources of information – current and historical – so that they remain accessible for use at all times.

14 Ensure preservation of the organization's 'memory' in the form of its know-ledge base [2]

15 Provide appropriate education and training to enable all members of staff to meet their responsibilities in using knowledge and information.

16 Develop and apply reliable means of assessing the costs and value of informa tion, and the contribution it makes to achieving our objectives.

17 Provide appropriate human and financial resources for managing and developing the use of information and knowledge.

1 The Institute of Information Scientists (1998) has recently published helpful draft guidelines for professional ethics.

2 For a useful review of thinking about 'organizational memory', *see* Stein (1995):
...organizational memory concerns the knowledge-base of the organization ... the means by which knowledge from the past is brought to bear on present activities ... An improved organizational memory can benefit the organization in several ways:
• It can help managers maintain strategic direction over time.
• It can help the organization avoid the nightmare of cycling through old solutions to new problems because no one can remember what was done before.
• It can give new meaning to the work of individuals if such efforts are retained.
• It can facilitate organizational learning.
• It can strengthen the identity of the organization.
• It can provide newcomers with access to the expertise of those who preceded them.

18 Seek to use knowledge and information to support the management of change and the development of change initiatives to benefit the organization, and to create new knowledge.[3]

19 Use this policy as the basis for information strategies to support our business strategy.

Appendices:
● The definition of information for this organization (a brief statement of what constitutes information from the point of view of the organization's goals) ● Its information resources (a list of the resources it holds and maintains to support its use of knowledge and information in achieving its goals).

Nailing down the basic principles

We cannot afford to let even the broadest statement of an information policy be in such general terms that everyone can assent to it and nobody feels under any obligation to do anything about it. The policy statement has to nail down the principles in a way that commits the organization to doing something sensible that will be of benefit to it where most needed. This example, from an actual organization (the subject of a case study in Orna, 1990, p281), shows one instance of doing it. The organization made its living by analysing the advertisements in trade and technical and consumer periodicals, and selling reports based on the analysis to publishers and editors in this area of the industry as a guide to what the competition was doing. At the time of the information audit whose findings are described in Table 5.1 (*see* p97), it was in some trouble.

So the principles about getting information on time and in the right format to the users, training in the appropriate information skills, and information interchange were expressed in terms of:
● Defining the key production jobs to take account of the information-based nature of the organization's activities ● Establishing appropriate measures of quality control ● Promoting the necessary flows of information, and communication within and between different functions ● Providing appropriate training for staff, supported by self-help training and reference products.

Again, if the mapping of the findings of the audit on to the organization's objectives has shown that failures to communicate essential information between different parts of the organization are hindering the achievement of objectives, then the information policy statement should emphasize bringing together staff from different areas to explain their work and information needs to one another, and to negotiate how to promote information interchange.

As a final example, the ways in which the organization tells its markets or its public about what it has to offer, or gives its staff the information they need to do their jobs, may emerge as a crucial area for success and a current cause of failures. In that case, the information policy objective of getting information in the right format to those who need to use it should be formulated to put emphasis on such activities as analysing the target markets for its information products, relating them to their role in meeting its objectives, and applying appropriate expertise to develop products that meet the needs of users.

3 *See* Nonaka and Takeuchi (1995) and Choo (1996).

Key objectives	Findings
To deliver reports to clients to the agreed schedule and at required level of accuracy	Neither timing nor accuracy requirements being met because: • Information about clients' requirements badly managed • Nature of data analysis tasks not understood by management; staff doing it did not understand its significance; no training in principles of indexing, which in fact is essence of the job • No standards for day-to-day communication of information • No adequate procedures for schedule maintenance • No standards for quality control
To sell the company's products to new clients, and ensure that existing ones stay with the company	Little difficulty in selling the products, because there is a recognized need for them, but a lot of difficulty in keeping existing clients, for the reasons indicated above
To support production and product development with an efficient and effective computer system	• Problems of interface between users and the system (and the system manager), lack of training • Software not appropriate for the job Hardware, especially printers, not up to requirements; liable to disastrous breakdown

Table 5.1
Example of key objectives and the findings from an information audit

Who drafts the policy?

Given the emphasis on continuity and maintaining the flow of action, it is sensible for whatever grouping has managed the stages which have led to this point to take responsibility for drafting the information policy. If there has been a steering group, for example, it would become their next responsibility, and they would delegate the actual drafting to the individual(s) or group who ran the audit or other earlier initiatives. The brief for the draft should be on these lines:
• Short • Clearly linked to what the organization is trying to do, where it is seeking to go • Focused on key points • Providing a framework on which people can grow their ideas based on their knowledge and experience • Expressed in ways appropriate for its character and culture • Visually well designed and accessible.

Existing structures developed for information auditing will allow for discussion of the draft with 'management champions' who can prepare the ground for its presentation to the top management team. This is a stage which should be completed as quickly as is consistent with due consideration, because it marks a 'milestone' in the journey towards strategic use of information and knowledge, and because the output is a tangible and saleable product.

Benefits	Leads to ...
Integration of all information activities	Information can make its full contribution to meeting organizational objectives
Decision making on resources for information activities can be objective, because it's based on the organization's objectives and priorities	Effective deployment of resources; long-term planning becomes possible; continuity in developing use of information promoted, and wasted investment avoided
Co-operation among those responsible for managing information resources, and between them and stakeholders, is promoted	Enriched use of knowledge and information through inter-functional and inter-disciplinary co-operation; reduced unproductive time on dog-in-a-manger behaviour; discovery of new possibilities for productive use of knowledge and information
Enhanced chances of successful innovation and competition	Improved return on R&D investment, increased market share, better competitive position
Sound decisions on investment in IT and systems	IT and systems support information objectives; systems permit productive developments in information use; promote internal and external information interactions; support people in using knowledge and information; upgrading of skills; increased job satisfaction
Constant internal and environmental monitoring and intelligence gathering makes possible anticipation of change, flexible response, and productive change can be used to plan change initiatives	Information activities continue to be appropriate for what the organization seeks to achieve; new situations can be evaluated on the basis of knowledge; threats avoided; information initiatives

Table 5.2
Long-term benefits from an information policy

Selling the policy

In this and subsequent stages of the journey, the earlier investment of time in establishing working groups, reporting structures and protocols begins to pay off. It doesn't have to be done again! And the structures created at the beginning will have been enriched and strengthened by the experience of shared work, and by the links and interchanges developed during the work throughout the organization. There is rather less explaining to do; it starts to become possible to refer back to ideas that have started to take root in the organizational compost. And there should be some attractive if small benefits already gained, as well as the prospect of future ones, as an incentive to buy into the next stages of the process.

The benefits are substantial ones; they can be summarized as shown in Table 5.2.

Presentation

Once again, as with the results of the information audit, presentation both upwards and outwards, to top management and branching outward into the organization is essential; and in this case it is even more important to pull out all the stops and make an impressive job of it. The fact that the foundations have been laid, and that the audience have absorbed some of the key ideas and know the people involved, makes it a rather easier task, and so does the fact that the product is a compact one.

With top management the main aim is to get them to sign up to the policy, to write a reference to it into corporate objectives as an essential element in them, and to accept it as the basis for further development of organizational information strategy. Perhaps the most creative and valuable results can come from presenting the policy outwards into the organization, and using it as an 'educational product'. It can form the basis for group discussions, focusing on specific points of the policy, in which people look at the policy in relation to their own work and interpret it creatively in the light of their own knowledge and experience, start negotiating with one another over information use, and commit themselves to participating in information strategy development, which is the real engine that will drive the organization's progress to full and productive use of its information and knowledge resources.

The policy as a foundation for information strategy

Looking at the policy in this way, in relation to key business objectives, and especially to the changes in orientation which it seeks to make, will give indicators of focal points for information strategy development (*see* pp107–109), just as considering what the organization is and does suggests what an information audit should look at.

Figure 5.1 (*see* over), shows the path we have travelled so far, a spiral one which starts from understanding the organization's aspirations and character; goes on to define what, in the light of them, it should be doing with knowledge and information; matches that against what it is really doing, through information auditing; and uses the output to refine its ideas about how it should use knowledge and information, into an information policy. That policy in turn will form another 'landing' on the route towards information strategy which expresses the policy in actions directed towards achieving its aims over defined periods of time.

Summary

● Finalizing an organizational information policy and getting it accepted is an essential first follow-up to an information audit, and it should be done speedily, on the principle of striking while the iron is hot ● A wide range of commitments *can* go into the policy ● But it is for the people in the organization to use the knowledge gained so far to decide what is feasible for *their* policy and how to formulate it ● The policy should be drafted by those who have done the preliminary work of organizational analysis and information auditing ● It should make a compact and attractive product for selling throughout the organization ● In planning presentation, use the structures and contacts built during the audit ● In presenting the policy, sell it on quick wins already achieved through using information, and on long-term benefits

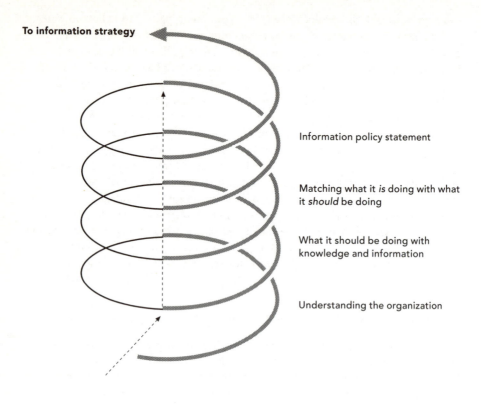

To information strategy

Information policy statement

Matching what it *is* doing with what it *should* be doing

What it should be doing with knowledge and information

Understanding the organization

Figure 5.1
The path we have travelled so far

to come ● The aim of presenting the policy upwards is to get top management to sign up to it and what follows from it – information strategy development; the aim of presenting it outwards is to get people to enrich it with their knowledge and experience, and to join in developing information strategy.

References
Choo, C. W. (1996), 'The knowing organization; how organizations use information to construct meaning, create knowledge and make decisions', *International Journal of Information Management*, 16 (5), 329–340.
Davenport, T. H. with Prusak, L. (1997), *Information Ecology Mastering the information and knowledge environment*. New York: Oxford University Press.
Institute of Information Scientists. (1998), 'Draft IIS Guidelines for professional ethics for information professionals', *Inform*, January/February, 4–6.
Nonaka, I. and Takeuchi, H. (1995), *The Knowledge-creating Company*, New York: Oxford University Press.
Orna, E. (1990), *Practical Information Policies*, Aldershot: Gower.
Stein, E. W. (1995), 'Organizational memory: Review of concepts and recommendations for management', *International Journal of Information Management*, 15 (2), 17–32.

Practical insights

Relevant recent experience

One of the main recommendations from the recent information audit described earlier in detail (*see* Chapters 3.2 and 4.2), was an organizational information policy. The findings from the audit (*see* pp84–86) are relevant to most of the policy points suggested on pp94–96, which could be used as a framework in formulating a policy in specific terms appropriate to the organization (as discussed on p96).

The good communication practice set up during that audit, with speedy reporting back to each department and discussion of ideas for action (*see* Chapter 4.2 pp83–84) makes a good basis for presenting information policy directly.

A final practical point on the basis of recent experience. Many organizations still lack a single authoritative repository of their policies managed by someone with this as their specific responsibility; different versions float around in various places, and there is no one point of reference for the current authorized version – a dangerous state of affairs. If you have encountered it in your own organization, then the information policy should include establishing a policies repository, and it can be the first item in the repository.

Moving from policy to strategy: key themes

The chapter you have just read ends with discussing information policy as the foundation for organizational information strategy; the next chapter is about developing and using an information strategy. In moving from policy to strategy, we need to think hard about some main concerns of information strategy, and about how they relate to the organization for which the strategy is intended. They are:
- Why organizations need to integrate their use of information, knowledge and technology with the way human beings interact in the organization • The real value that organizations get from information – how it contributes to success
- Why organizations need to apply knowledge and information to deal successfully with change • Why knowledge management and information management are mutually dependent and both are necessary for successful action • What information and knowledge strategy should do for organizations.

The present book is meant to be a short, practical, introductory one, but I should be failing in my obligations to readers if I skipped over themes which are so fundamental to successful practical management of knowledge and information. The people responsible for developing information strategy, and those with any kind of responsibility for managing knowledge and information, have to be advocates and interpreters of these ideas, in order to get support and resources for doing the job.

I don't, however, want to hold up the overview of the process at this point; so we shall explore these important and interesting topics in Chapter 7.

Developing and using an information strategy

Seven key words for strategic thinking:
1 Differentiation – *what makes the organization unique.* 2 Concentration – *on priorities: strengths, weaknesses, opportunities, threats.* 3 Repercussions – *how one strategic activity can lead to other possibilities for future action.* 4 Timing – *using information to take change initiatives at the right time.* 5 Momentum – *keeping up the initiative once it's started.* 6 Imbalance – *'an unbalanced strategy that shakes up an organization is best for its long-term health'.* 7 Combination – *interdependence of all the resources of the organization, so it implies integrated management of information.*
–Based on ITAMI, HIROYUKI with ROEHL, THOMAS, W. (1987), p169

> *Information strategy also means making choices, not carving out a master plan in stone.*
> –DAVENPORT, T. (1997), p46

Definitions and distinctions

This chapter moves on to the practicalities of the process of creating an organizational strategy for using knowledge and information. Before we begin, a reminder, to save you having to turn back to the start of the book, of the relevant definitions and distinctions.

Organizational information strategy

Information strategy is the detailed expression of information policy in terms of objectives, targets, and actions to achieve them, for a defined period ahead. Information strategy provides the framework for the management of information. Information strategy, contained within the framework of an organizational policy for information and supported by appropriate systems and technology, is the 'engine' for:
● Maintaining, managing and applying the organization's information resources
● Supporting its essential knowledge base and all who contribute to it, with strategic intelligence[1], for achieving its key business objectives.

[1] 'Strategic intelligence can ... be defined as follows: it is what a company needs to know about its business environment to enable it to anticipate change and design appropriate strategies that will create business value for customers and be profitable in new markets and industries in the future. ... The value of strategic intelligence comes from improving the capabilities of managers and workers in a company to learn about changes in the business or industry environment which will require rethinking business practices. They must then share their perceptions, new information and insights wherever in the company such information is needed. The challenge for strategic intelligence is to increase the "intelligence quotient" of all managers and employees in a company ...' (Marchand 1997a)

Distinctions

Information policy:
• At the level of principles • Short statement • Can be developed at one go
• Meant to last.
Information strategy:
• Basis for action for a given period • Reviewed at frequent intervals • Can be
developed and implemented in stages.
Information systems/IT strategy:
• Depends on what information the organization needs, and how it needs to
use it • Deals with applications software and infrastructure to support informa-
tion management • Decisions on information policy and strategy have to
come first.

The engine of change and development

As Figure 6.1 (*see* p104) suggests, a strong information strategy, which is well understood and has the commitment of everyone in the organization, can become the
engine that:
• Drives interchanges of information internally and with outside world • Brings
in intelligence about change • Leads to integrated responses • Promotes creation
of new knowledge through internal interactions • Leads to initiatives, directed
both internally and to outside world, which make for success in innovation and
competition.

The baseline – what you need to know before starting

Here we need to remind ourselves of what was said in Chapter 2 about laying the
foundations for the strategic use of information and knowledge.

The identity of the organization

What is its primary orientation? Is it, for example, towards:
• The market and customers? • Risk avoidance? • Cost reduction? • Innovation?
   If it is currently seeking to adopt a new orientation, as many organizations today,
for example, are trying to become customer-focused, then that factor is of particular
significance for the kind of strategy it will need to support it in the attempt.
   What is its information culture? Is the emphasis on communicating and building relationships? On influencing and controlling? On problem solving and effi-
ciency? Or on discovery, inquiry, innovation?
   Does it proclaim its dedication to 'information sharing'? And if it does, how
does that go down in practice? Are people willing to interact and negotiate over
the information resources they hold, or do they clutch them firmly and growl at
strangers who approach? What of its 'information politics'? Do they fall into any
of the categories that Davenport and his co-authors (1992) identify? (*see* Chapter 2).
   What are its key objectives, and the priorities among them? (*see* Table 6.1 on p105).

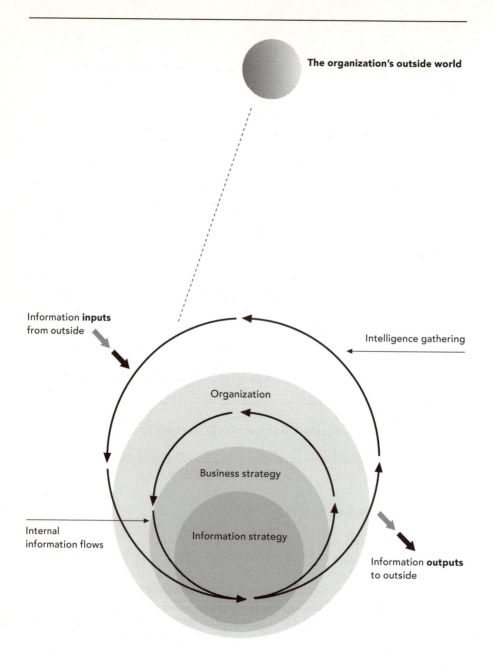

The organization's outside world

Information **inputs** from outside

Intelligence gathering

Organization

Business strategy

Information strategy

Internal information flows

Information **outputs** to outside

Figure 6.1
Information strategy, the engine

'What should be' with respect to knowledge and information

Next we need to answer (as we did in Tables 2.1 and 2.2, pp21–25 and Table 2.3 pp27–32) these questions about the knowledge and information implications of what the organization claims it is trying to do:

● What does it need to know to achieve its objectives? ● What information does it need to maintain its knowledge?

That gives a picture of 'what should be', against which, as recommended in Chapter 3, the information audit can start finding out 'what is', in terms of information resources, where they are, what they consist of, who are their guardians and stakeholders, how they are used, and how well they support what the organization is trying to do.

The output from all that questioning and finding answers provides the material on which the information strategy developer has to work. Fortunately, if an information audit has been carried out, it should be well structured as a result of the work done on it in the course of interpreting and presenting the findings, and therefore accessible and manageable. And if the people responsible for the audit are also involved, as they should be, in strategy development, they will have an invaluable structure of knowledge and be able to move swiftly about it, and identify priorities.

Technocratic Utopianism	A heavily technical approach to information management stressing categorization and modeling of an organization's full information assets, with heavy reliance on emerging technologies
Anarchy	The absence of any overall information management policy, leaving individuals to obtain and manage their own information.
Feudalism	The management of information by individual business units or functions, which define their own information needs and report only limited information to the overall corporation.
Monarchy	The definition of information categories and reporting structures by the firm's leaders, who may or may not share the information willingly after collecting it.
Federalism	An approach to information management based on consensus and negotiation on the organization's key information elements and reporting structures.

Table 6.1
Models of Information Politics. From Davenport et al (1992)

Whose business is information strategy?

Information strategy is intended to benefit the whole organization in its most critical activities, and so its development needs to draw on a wide range of knowledge and experience.

1 Managers of information resources, for example:
- Environmental intelligence • Customer information • Competitor information • Economic/financial information • Human resources • Information service/library/archives (these resources often seem to be overlooked when projects of this kind are being set up; but the people in charge of them don't have to accept invisibility!) [2]
- Marketing • Membership • Contacts • R&D • Information products
2 Managers of information systems and information technology
3 Stakeholders in information resources
4 Managers responsible for the organization's corporate strategy.

Essential resources

The essential resources are similar to those needed for an information audit (they are listed briefly below as a reminder). If a properly resourced audit has been carried out in the organization, the structures, reporting arrangements, groupings and relationships in the course of that process can be built on. (Another instance of the value of setting things up properly first time round – the cost and effort next time is minimized.)

Essentials for information strategy development are:
- A compact representative group to manage it (drawing on the constituencies mentioned above) • Knowledge of the organization • Top management support • Understanding throughout the organization of what is being done • 'Management champion' • Straightforward reporting arrangements • A clear brief • Realistic phased timetable • Appropriate resources of time and finance.

Other enabling conditions for success

Nonaka and Takeuchi (1995) put forward some conditions as enablers of knowledge creation. The first of them is a strategy for knowledge and information, which is what is currently occupying our attention; the next a vision of the kind of knowledge the organization needs, which has been discussed in Chapter 3; and the third a management system to implement the strategy for achieving the vision. The others are worth citing in some detail here, because I think they are both a help in developing information strategy, and something which it should seek to promote and keep in being throughout the organization. In quoting them, I shall intersperse some real-life stories from the case studies and elsewhere.

2 Bonaventura (1997) – who works for a systems company – puts the case for their presence, and that of other essential contributors, emphatically: 'While the technology is non-trivial, it will not make or break a Knowledge Management programme: the human support infrastructure (librarians, publishers, design teams) will ... any methodology which is targeting Knowledge Management needs to address the definition and installation of that support infrastructure.'

• The first of these enablers is maximum possible autonomy for the individuals and teams to whom the organization entrusts responsibility for new developments; this allows original ideas to develop and spread through the organization, upwards, downwards and sideways, and is part of the process described in Japanese management thinking as 'middle-up-down management'.

> ... knowledge is created by middle managers, who are often leaders of a team or task force, through a spiral conversion process involving both the top and the front-line employees ... The process puts middle managers at the very center of knowledge management, positioning them at the intersection of the vertical and horizontal flows of information with the company.
> (Nonaka and Takeuchi, 1995, p127)

The case study of the Surrey Police Force (in Orna, 1999) provides an example. As described in the case study, action which led to the development of an information policy and strategy came about in that way, when ideas originating from an individual were given the opportunity of spreading upwards and outwards into the organization.

The next enabler is cross-functional teams, drawing in people from a broad cross section of different organizational activities.

Finally, Nonaka and Takeuchi recommend what is described as 'fluctuation and creative chaos', designed to 'stimulate the interaction between the organization and the external environment'. This is important because it introduces discontinuity, and the opportunity to reconsider values through dialogue and interaction. Such an alternation of order and chaos is not seen as something to be afraid of. The concept is very different from Western 'problem solving'; it demands the 'purposeful use of ambiguity', and can succeed only when members of the organization 'have the ability to reflect upon their actions'. It can lead to questioning of values as well as of factual premises.[3] This can take place only in a supportive environment, not in the kind of chaos which is brought on by panic and authoritarianism. It demands great self-confidence on the part of management to seek to promote this as part of organizational development, but I suspect it happens spontaneously and to good effect in the course of many projects such as those described in the case studies. Certainly these unfamiliar ideas underline the importance of allowing time for thinking and insisting that people do think, instead of the usual tacit assumption that thinking is not working, and that you have to show you're working by rushing around

Where to start – focal points for strategy development

It is not possible or desirable to develop the strategy everywhere at once; as with information auditing, the 'spiral' approach, in which development and implementation interact, and in which at each turn there can be learning and diffusion further into the organization, is recommended (see below, p110). So a choice has to be made of the points where application of an information strategy will bring most effect.

---

3 See also Itami and Roehl (1987) on 'imbalance', as cited at the start of this chapter: the thinking here is that there should be periods when resources and talents are not in balance with current strategy; the organization should not be in equilibrium for too long or it loses momentum; it needs to progress through zigzags.

As Marchand (1997b) reminds us, when organizations invest for information management, they should concentrate on the distinctive, innovative end of their activities because that is where the return on investment is potentially higher (in contrast, most IT investment is still at the conventional end, where the return is lower). So we need to look for the organization's:

● Strengths ● Unique features ● Core competencies (the distinctive ones, what the organization is very good at, those of highest potential value to it) ● Survival essentials (including what the organization is not very good at, and areas where this constitutes a risk) ● Potential for innovation.

Examples of actual starting points

Some of these examples are drawn from the case studies in Orna, 1999, others from the recent experience of other organizations. Among them, they cover in a variety of ways the key concerns of: people in relation to technology; change; and the value of knowledge and information.

Getting the benefits of informal information interchange, without the disadvantages of once-only use

An international charity; its information strategy aims at:
● *Combining informal email networks with more permanent databases, using IT to make it easy to contribute knowledge from the informal exchanges to a sophisticated database which allows multiple use* ● *Counteracting the weakness of project-centred working by making sure that knowledge and information from projects – and especially the lessons of what worked and what failed – are managed and made accessible for future use. This is a frequently encountered problem today, and part of the strategic solution may lie in structural change; if an organization's structure is solely task-force and project-based, there are dangers of information loss because it is not appropriate for transferring the knowledge gained during projects into a robust and durable knowledge base. Nonaka and Takeuchi (1995) propose a 'hypertext organization' in which different 'layers' coexist. When projects are completed, 'members move down to the knowledge-base layer and make an inventory of the knowledge created and/or acquired', including successes and failures.*

Helping staff to be aware of their own knowledge and of its value in interaction with the knowledge of others in the organization.

A specialist insurance company; its strategy aims at making it part of the job description of its highly qualified staff to contribute to the business's knowledge base,[4] so that colleagues and clients can use it to grow the business. The strategy involves intensive use of quite sophisticated technology, and investment in education for staff in using it.

4 An observation in this context; today a number of organizations are both seeking integrated information management, and trying to get all managers to adopt information management as part of their job responsibilities. These are both reasonable things to do, but there seems to be an as yet unresolved problem of how to combine decentralized management of information with an overview of what is going on and a co-ordinated strategy. The solution will demand some crafty work on structure and culture, and ingenious support from systems and technology.

Integrated management of all information resources

A large museum; the focus for developing its information strategy is integrated use of the whole range of its information resources, which will, for example, allow staff planning multimedia products for sale to draw on information about the collections, potential markets, visitors, possible commercial partners and competing products.

Managing and using information from the organization's outside world

An international organization; it is strong on output of information, but has diagnosed a weakness in its failure to make enough use of the response which it gets from customers, clients, the public and government bodies. The focal point of its strategy development is managing incoming information so as to learn from it, plan action and develop policies.

The Australian Securities and Investments Commission (for the full story, *see* Orna, 1999, p197)

An exercise of 'information discovery' (information auditing) in the organization and development of an information policy resulted in a Strategic Information Plan which used the findings to propose seven key strategies:
1 Build an effective national information management framework of policy, planning, standards and collaboration.
2 Systematically identify and articulate core business information needs.
3 Improve business information processes and corporate data quality.
4 Develop an integrated information management structure for both electronic and physical documents and records.
5 Research and develop expertise to apply knowledge management tools and techniques.
6 Ensure that operational staff are able to make effective use of information resources.
7 Leverage use of the Internet.

Amnesty International (for the full story *see* Orna, 1999, p186)

The focal points for developing an international information management strategy include:
● Integrating the use of IT and the use of information ● Improving the quality of decisions on investment in IT to benefit users in countries with few resources ● Testing the effectiveness of what the organization does with information.

Surrey Police Force (for the full story, *see* Orna, 1999, p325)

Here the information strategy is driven by the need to use information economically, to avoid multiple inputs, to standardize, and to develop a system that allows each element of information to be accessed and used in multiple contexts. Its aim is fully integrated management of information, with maximum access and maximum openness. This approach has led to changes in organizational structure, which bring together, in one information services department, systems, information technology, library, records, and registry.

The develop–implement–learn spiral

If the people responsible for developing information strategy were to try to get it complete in every detail before starting to use it, they would never see it applied.

'Analysis paralysis' would set in, with its trail of talk, working parties, reports, heaps of documents, disillusion, all to be finally forgotten as yet another failed initiative.

So it is wise not to think of it as an end-on process of first develop, then implement. It is only by doing something that you find out if what you have planned really works. Equally, it is no good doing something unless you make sure to learn the lessons and to pass them on. That is the reasoning behind proposing interaction between developing the strategy and putting it into action. I envisage it as a spiral process, with learning at each turn of the spiral, and new people being drawn into development as it continues. It is a rotating spiral, as well, which means that there is a constant process of revisiting earlier stages to monitor and update (*see* Figure 6.2).

This prototyping approach also gives the best chance of the strategy being understood and integrated into the way the organization sets about its business; it

- Allows you to demonstrate
  - *without taking too long about it,*
    - *or tying up too many resources,*
      - *real benefits of applying a strategic approach to information*
      - *in areas that are critical for the organization;*
    - *to measure the impact at the end of each phase;*
  - *and to learn more each time around.*

As suggested earlier, it is not reasonable to expect immediate and full understanding at the top level (as Marchand,1997b says, general managers are accustomed to managing *with* information, but the management *of* information is as yet a rather unfamiliar concept). Experience shows that a long time is needed for such ideas to take root in the thinking of senior managers, but it is time well spent, because it can ensure that they will contribute to developing the strategy for the areas of business which they control and know well, and will take good advantage of it. And the moral of that is to keep at it; understanding will grow as the strategy is put into effect; and the day will come when top management will start taking credit for it and even boasting of it! (For further encouragement, read Davenport's outstanding book on *Information Ecology* (1997); the chapter on information strategy recommends a similar approach to the one advocated here, backed up by Davenport's wide range of experience.)

What the organization stands to gain

Meantime, no opportunity should be lost of selling the benefits of the integrated management of knowledge and information in the framework of a strategy which is contained within the organization's overall corporate strategy.

Integrated management of knowledge and information

- Helps organizations learn from experience • Keeps their knowledge in good form for application • Allows them to take advantage of opportunities • Helps them to avoid dangers by awareness of change • Supports them in innovating, redefining problems, finding new solutions • Helps them gain, and keep, reputation • Gives a sound basis for resource allocation • Provides a strong framework

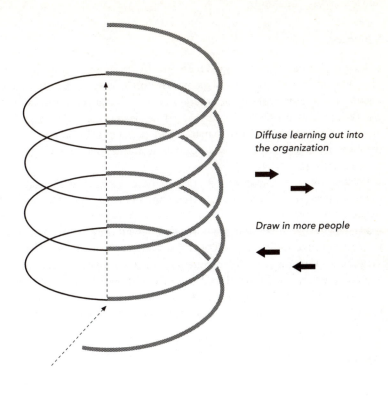

Diffuse learning out into the organization

Draw in more people

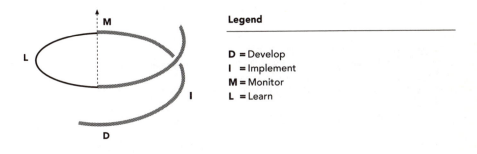

Legend

D = Develop
I = Implement
M = Monitor
L = Learn

Figure 6.2
Spiral of develop–implement–monitor–learn

for IS/IT strategy ● Makes a basis for assessing the business value that information and knowledge contribute.

Summary

● A strong information strategy can become the engine of successful change and development for organizations ● Before starting to develop it, you need to know about: ○ Your organization's orientation ○ Its information culture ○ Its key objectives and priorities ● You also need to know how well what it actually does with information and knowledge matches what it should be doing – preferably through an information audit ● Information strategy development needs co-operative effort from:

○ Managers of all the organization's information resources ○ The stakeholders in them ○ Managers of information systems and information technology ○ Managers responsible for corporate strategy ● It needs a compact group to manage it, a management champion, understanding throughout the organization, and proper resources of time and money ● Other things that help: a self-organizing team with maximum autonomy; acknowledgement of the importance of thinking, and time for it ● Strategy can't be developed everywhere at once; it's better to choose significant focal points for development, and work by a spiral of develop–implement–learn. That way, at each turn there can be learning, diffusion into the organization, and drawing in of new people.

References

BONAVENTURA, M. (1997), 'The benefits of a knowledge culture', *Aslib Proceedings*, 49 (4) 82–89.

DAVENPORT, T. H., ECCLES, R. G. and PRUSAK, L. (1992), 'Information politics', *Sloan Management Review*, Fall, 53–65.

DAVENPORT, T. H. with PRUSAK, L. (1997), *Information Ecology. Mastering the information and knowledge environment*, New York: Oxford University Press.

ITAMI, H. with ROEHL, T. W. (1987) , *Mobilizing Invisible Assets*, Boston, MA: Harvard University Press.

MARCHAND, D. A. (1997a), 'Managing strategic intelligence', *Financial Times Mastering Management*, London: Financial Times/Pitman.

MARCHAND, D. A . (1997b), 'Competing with information: know what you want', *FT Mastering Management Reader*, July/August, 7–12.

NONAKA, I. and TAKEUCHI, H. (1995), *The Knowledge-creating Company: how Japanese companies create the dynamics of information*, New York: Oxford University Press.

ORNA, E. (1999), *Practical information Policies*, Ed2, Aldershot: Gower.

Practical insights

'Information orientation' – A context for information strategy

The focus here is research reported in a recent book – *Information Orientation* (Marchand et al 2002). The authors started with the research question: 'Is there a comprehensive measure of effective information use that predicts business performance?' They concluded, after studying the thinking of a large international sample of over 1000 top-level managers on these topics, that they had, for the first time, established the nature of the relationship between information use and business performance, and that they had been able to create a comprehensive measure. In doing so, they have taken a large step towards resolving the intractable problem of finding an acceptable measure of the value that using knowledge and information creates for organizations.

At the same time, their research provides a sound context within which to develop information strategies. The context is the interlocking of:
● IT practices ● Information management practices ● Information behaviour and values (sometimes described as organizational information culture) to form an integrated 'Information Orientation' relevant to the organization's business goals.

It is a sound context, because the research indicates that business performance depends on such an orientation – organizations 'must achieve competence and synergy across all three information capabilities ... as a precondition to achieving superior business performance' – it is not enough to be good at each element in isolation; they have to work together and support one another in achieving organizational goals.

Support for the information auditing approach

The argument that mutual support and interaction among IT, information management, and information behaviour/culture is essential if the use of information is to add business value for organizations fits very well with the approach to information auditing advocated in this book. That approach looks at precisely those 'information capabilities' and how they work with (or against) one another in actuality, as compared with what should be happening in these domains.

The value of the work by Marchand and his colleagues is that it provides a strong research-based underpinning – derived from the thinking of top managers in a range of businesses and organizations – for the practice- and experience–based outcomes from information audits. Their findings about that thinking, summarized below, give useful pointers to relative strengths and weaker points in senior managers' perceptions, and can be a valuable guide in planning the approach to information-strategy development (for useful arguments based on this research, *see* Chapter 7, pp133–135).

IT practices

The senior managers proved to have a sophisticated concept of IT practices; and they did not believe that good IT practices alone are sufficient to improve business performance; they viewed them as a necessary, but not sufficient, condition.

They distinguished all these levels of IT support:
- for management decision making • for innovation • for business processes
- for operational activities.

The 'maturity model' used in the research indicates that these levels form a kind of ladder, up which organizations move on their way to information maturity, starting from the bottom rung of IT in support of operational activities; the most mature organizations attach most significance to the top two.

Information management practices

The managers in the study distinguished these information-management processes:
- Sensing (exercising awareness of developments in the environment on which it is vital for the organization to be well informed) • Collecting • Organizing
- Processing • Maintaining.

Some were less familiar to them than others. Sensing in particular was 'not as well formulated' in their minds – how you sense, what you need to sense, seem less clearly grasped, and there was especially low understanding of the need for sensing economic, political, and social changes affecting businesses.

Here too, there was 'no evidence indicating that managers believe this information capability alone has a profound effect on business performance', and the analysis points to an understanding of its 'close inter-relationship with IT practices'

Information behaviours/values

The researchers observe that this area has not been the object of structured and measurable management activities; nor yet has improving people's behaviours and values as regards information use been seen as part of the IT and information management functions. They also remark that it is not easy to develop proactive information behaviour (in which people willingly take information initiatives be- cause they see them as of benefit to themselves as well as others), because it depends on other interdependent information behaviours and values. These behaviours and values and their inter-relations are:

Integrity

Of information, and of the context of its use. The foundation for good information use, guaranteeing that information is truthful, accurate and without bias, it sets 'appropriate boundaries for ethical information behavior' and influences directly 'the formal use of information within an organization' (Marchand et al p102).

Formal information sources

If organizations can give first place to formal information sources rather than informal ones, they will improve the reliability and quality of their information.

Whether they are able to do so depends on integrity as defined above. People will be readier to make information explicit and available in formal sources when they share and trust the same values about appropriate information use.

Information control

The definition of this term used in the research is not the traditional 'top-down' one, but a modern 'bottom-up' interpretation in terms of managers using performance-based information to motivate people to relate their own personal performance to the organization's business performance: 'By linking individual performance to organizational performance, managers could directly motivate employees, creating proactive information behaviors for improved information effectiveness' (Marchand et al p103).

Transparency

Treating 'errors, mistakes, failures, and surprises as constructive learning opportunities' (Marchand et al p103). The researchers believe that this kind of behaviour is directly influenced by information control as defined above, supported by integrity and formal information use. If managers share trustworthy formalized information about the organization's performance with staff, they help create a more transparent and open environment, where mistakes and failures can be dealt with constructively. Such transparency in information use encourages the much talked of but less often practised behaviour of information sharing.

Sharing

If there is transparency as defined above in the organization, it allows senior managers to build trust in sharing information. If organization members are able to deal positively with mistakes, errors and failures (information of the kind that touches individual feelings most closely), then they will be more disposed to share other kinds of information that involve less personal risk, and that directly influences proactive behaviour. Sharing is also directly influenced by information control: 'If senior managers provide formal, credible and useful information about the performance of the company at each level of employees, they can build a climate of trust' that leads to 'a form of "enlightened self-interest" that promotes the attitude that people share because it is in their best interests to share information that can improve decision making and make the company less prone to errors, mistakes, failures, and surprises' (Marchand et al p104).

Senior managers in the research perceived these features as components of information behaviour and values, and they appeared to 'implicitly understand' that information behaviour and values have to be supported by 'solid IT practices' and 'competent IM practices' – ie those focused on contributing to effective information use, which in turn impacts on business performance – if they are to contribute to substantial improvement in business performance.

It would be encouraging to think that all the chief executives who promote a 'vision' of information sharing, openness, transparency, etc to 'their people' have this kind of understanding, but experience suggests it is unlikely. Yet abusing these values by preaching them from the top but practising the reverse leads to degrading business performance, and in the worst case to collapse and irreparable loss of reputation. The sorry trail of corporate wrongdoing, based on deliberate flouting of information integrity, and ultimate exposure initiated by the Enron case should act as an awful warning of where it leads.

Reference

MARCHAND, D., KETTINGER, W. and ROLLINS, J. (2002), *Information Orientation. The link to business performance*, Oxford: Oxford University Press.

Thinking allowed!
Ideas and arguments

The mere presence of technology won't create a learning organization,
a meritocracy, or a knowledge-creating company.
– T. H. DAVENPORT and L. PRUSAK (1998)

> *To put it bluntly, arriving at a value of information or knowledge*
> *is not an objective exercise.*
> – C. OPPENHEIM, J. STENSON and R. M. SWILSON (2002)

The purpose of this chapter

I wrote in the first chapter:
'A policy acquires value only when thinking human beings get together to put it to use. When that happens, it becomes a framework of reference, securely attached to the organization's business strategy, within which it can build strategies, standards, procedures, rules for how people use information and knowledge.'

Between that chapter and the present one, we have concentrated on the 'how to do it' aspects, the processes of creating information policies and strategies, though I hope without downplaying the 'why do it' element, for it is dishonest and dangerous to tell people what to do and how to do it without saying why they should do it and what results they can expect. Now, in this final chapter, I want to bring together the underlying ideas that inform the book, and to state them briefly and straightforwardly, without compromising their integrity. I make no apology for emphasizing ideas and thinking in a book that's billed as 'practical'. Thinking is one of the most practical, cost-effective, and low-risk activities that we can engage in; if there were more of it about we would all be in less trouble. Human beings advanced so rapidly because they are social creatures who found out how to think; and those who can think straight and honestly, explain their thinking, and convince others to join in acting on it have a natural advantage, and can do good to their fellows.

Organizational information policy and strategy are only worth having if the organization that has them uses them to move towards an information environment where people, supported by well-managed information resources and technology tools, can exchange and create knowledge and apply it to achieve desired change, do useful new things, and add value. To achieve that, those involved in developing the policies and strategies need to understand the central ideas thoroughly, keep them to the fore, and endeavour to spread understanding to the minds of the other people whose support is critical. They have to protect the gains made so far, and be ready to deal with all kinds of common situations in organizational life that can threaten them.

We have to realize that it takes a long time for unfamiliar ideas (and the ideas we are concerned with are unfamiliar to many worthy people at the top of many organizations) to take firm root. The process is rather like growing marram grass in sand dunes to stabilize ground that will otherwise shift with every wind that blows, so that over time a good soil will build up, able to sustain a rich variety of plants.

The story of Surrey Police (told in Orna, 1999, pp325–342) reveals that the process of developing a working information strategy there took a number of years, during which a senior manager sponsored the ideas of a member of his staff, who had put forward a first discussion paper on information strategy. The senior manager set up a high-level Information Management Steering Group and began a process of introducing members to the concepts of information strategy. There followed what looked like a protracted pause, during which they were described as 'discussing principles at length, but not initiating any projects' and leading to 'no discernible action'. However, in retrospect those concerned considered it time well spent because it had allowed senior managers to take ownership of the relevant ideas and to feel at home with them. The changed mind shift is described as from 'Why is it important and why should we do it?' to 'What should we do and how should we do it?' Once that had been achieved, progress was decisive and effective. It led to an 'Open Information Strategy' covering both information systems and information content, and then to a Knowledge Architecture combining these with emphasis on human resources. The results have helped the force towards fuller achievement of its objectives, by supporting staff in their work in the field with necessary information, and enabling them, through appropriate technological tools and training, to feed their own knowledge into the organization.

A similar story emerged from a research case study in the 1990s at The Tate Gallery (as Tate was then known). There it took from 1992 to 1999 to get to a comparable situation. The earlier stages of the process revealed mutual failures among different groups of staff to 'understand what information really is' and proved that 'the lessons of information awareness are very slow to learn', as those involved in the attempt put it; to their frustration, from one meeting to the next, senior managers lost their grip on ideas they appeared to have grasped. The perseverance of an alliance of information systems managers and information managers finally paid off, in a comprehensive strategy covering both information systems and information management, and the idea finally took root at top management level that there are measurable benefits to be had from managing information and having systems that support it. Since then, the gallery has developed a digital strategy 'framed within a developing information policy which sets out why the organization's information resources ... need to be treated with as much care as the works themselves. It also clarifies how an overview of those resources, a sharing approach, and attention to the management of information across the organisation as a whole, is essential to its future success.' (Beard et al 2001). The process that began so long ago has been the foundation for developments that will contribute to that success, including the creation of a comprehensive digital asset base, and partnerships to take forward new business opportunities.

So this chapter aims, on the basis of experience (my own, and that of other practitioners whom I respect), and on reliable research findings, to recapitulate the main underlying ideas, so that readers can make them their own, illuminate them with their own experience and knowledge, and use them in convincing, explaining, arguing a business case, answering objections, gaining allies, on the way towards developing and using information strategy. (The short final chapter which follows this one complements it with practical advice on dealing with typical organizational problems and obstacles that readers are likely to meet on the way through the processes described in the book.)

The themes are essentially those which I outlined briefly in Chapter 5 part 2 (*see* p101) and described as fundamental to successful practical management of knowledge and information:

● Why organizations need to integrate their use of information, knowledge and technology with the way human beings interact in the organization ● The real value that organizations get from information – how it contributes to their success ● How organizations can apply knowledge and information to deal with change and initiate successful change ● Why knowledge management and information management are mutually dependent and both are necessary for successful action.

Current thinking on all these themes is very relevant to information strategy, so at the end of each set of ideas and arguments, the lessons for information-strategy development are suggested, and at the end of this chapter they are all brought together so that readers can think about them in the light of their knowledge of their own organizations, and relate them to the practical issues of strategy development covered in Chapter 6.

Section 1
Integrating information, technology, and human interactions

This argument depends on four propositions. The first is simple and almost self-evident.

1 The purpose for which an organization is in business will determine the kind of things it needs to know about, and the know-how it needs, in order to succeed. So what constitutes vital knowledge will differ from organization to organization and will be highly specific to each one.

2 The second proposition relates to the definitions of knowledge and information adopted in this book (*see* pp7–8): to make a sound basis for action, the essential knowedge needs to be sustained and kept healthy with appropriate information, which the organization takes in from its own operations, and from the outside world that it depends on. What constitutes information for any organization is highly specific too, and organizations need to define it for themselves, in the light of what they seek to achieve.

3 The third proposition is based on the essential character of organizations (*see* pp 10–11, 15): since organizations are groupings of human beings, and since only human beings are capable of knowing and acting on what they know, their success in achieving their ends will depend not only on what they know and how they use information, but also on how the humans in the organization interact with one another inside the organization and with the outside world in using knowledge and information.

4 The fourth proposition is that success in achieving organizational ends will be influenced by how well the humans who make up the organization use the available technology to support their interactions in using knowledge and information. It has been relevant ever since we began our long relationship with the technologies that have shaped our consciousness, though it has been intensified to an extraordinary level by the arrival of computers.

Those propositions are the reason for the three key questions advocated in Chapter 2 (*see* Tables 2.1–2.3) to define what should be happening for success:

1 To achieve our objectives, what knowledge and/or know-how do we require?

2 What information do we need to draw on to maintain the knowledge we require?

3 Who are the people involved in using information, and what interactions and infomation flows are needed among them in order to transform it into knowledge and to act on it?

The answers to them in turn define what the organization should be doing with knowledge and information to succeed in its aims; they point to the 'information environment' it needs – the technology infrastructure, the information repositories, and the means of access to them – and to how people throughout the organization need to behave in using knowledge and information. That vision in turn forms the basis for investigating how close the real situation comes to it (as discussed in Chapters 3 and 4 on information auditing), and the results point to the nature and direction of the needed changes.

The propositions also imply the essential relationship that needs to exist among what organizations do with knowledge and information, the technology they use to support what they do, and the way they behave (organizational culture and values). If those things don't work together, they are unlikely to do much for the organization – which is the essence of the conclusion which Marchand and his colleagues (2002) reached in the research described earlier (Chapter 6 part 2, pp113–115), and discussed more fully later in this chapter (*see* p133): the better the mutual support among IT, information management and information behaviours and values – what they call 'Information Orientation' – the more the organization's use of information will contribute to its business performance.

Now we need to look at the arguments about two essential aspects of this theme:

1 Co-operation between information management and IT – between 'tools of the mind' and tools of technology

2 Human–human interaction and human–computer interaction in organizations.

How tools of the mind and tools of technology need to work together

The advance of the human mind has always been intimately connected with the tools we've invented to help us do the things we needed and wanted to do. Throughout our history there has been constant mutual influence between the two, each advance in the one leading to further development in the other, and the process seems to have speeded up with time.

McArthur (1986, p4) coined the phrase 'tools of the mind'; 'real tools', he wrote, 'have served as models for "tools of the mind" … The equipment that we handle in our daily lives has contributed to the enrichment of our minds, and this enrichment has further contributed to the enrichment of the equipment that we handle in our daily lives.' He distinguishes four critical stages in the progress of this mutual enrichment; as shown by Figure 7.1, each successive one has taken up much less time than its predecessor.

1 Consolidation of speech and gesture into language and oral traditions

2 Development of writing

3 Print

4 Electronic computers.

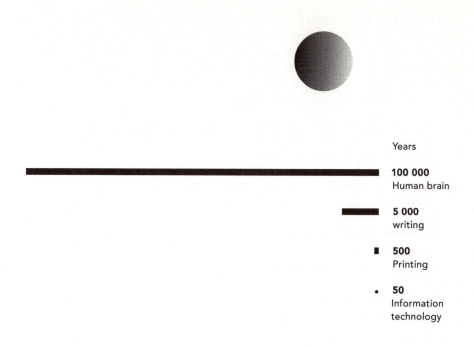

Figure 7.1
The timescale of human information storage

Years

100 000
Human brain

5 000
writing

500
Printing

50
Information
technology

As people came to engage more and more in intellectual work, the business of storing information outside the brain developed into what today we call information management, and led to the creation of tools of the mind to help them with the typical activities which Stibic (1980, pp3–4) describes: 'any professional in any field of science, technology or management, is involved to some extent … everyone has to plan and control his own work, everyone receives, stores and seeks information in different forms, everyone has to accept information by reading and listening, and everyone produces information in written and spoken form.' As McArthur's fascinating *Worlds of Reference* tells us, tools of the mind to help people do these things were created in classical Greece (the first encyclopedias); the Renaissance (the start of using alphabetical order, without which indexing wouldn't have got far); the Enlightenment (scientific taxonomy for grouping living organisms in 'families'); and the nineteenth – twentieth centuries (the great library classifications; thesauri; popular dictionaries).

And, at every step, tools of technology were developed to help in creating and using the tools of the mind. The rate at which they appeared speeded up over time, with the most rapid development from the early 1960s on, when 'the computer entered the field of the processing of non-numerical data', and started to reveal its extraordinary advantages of 'universality' (Stibic, 1980, p6) – its capacity to create an infinity of tools to support the things human beings want to do.

An example: taxonomy

The current interest in taxonomies for organizations makes a pertinent example of the proper relation between tools of the mind and technology tools. Today the term – much spoken of, but I suspect little understood by many who use it – is used to cover a range of tools and technological solutions for putting concepts relevant to the work of organizations into 'family' groups, categories, and hierarchies, in order to help in managing large stores of information.

> 'Classification esp. in relation to its general laws or principles; that department of science, or of a particular science or subject, which consists in or relates to classification.' (*Shorter Oxford Dictionary*)

> 'Structures that provide a way of classifying things – living organisms, products, books – into a series of hierarchical groups to make them easier to identify, study or locate. Taxonomies consist of two parts – structures and applications. Structures consist of the categories (or terms) themselves and the relationships that link them together. Applications are the navigation tools available to help users find information.' (Jean Graef, 2002)

The reasons why taxonomy is essential in scientific fields are concisely explained in the Oxford University Botanic Garden visitors' leaflet:

> 'A scientifically accurate system of grouping plants ... is vital for our survival as individuals and as a species.
> 1 Most of our plant-derived medicines come from species in just a few families. Trying to discover new drugs in plants without a good system of plant classification would be like looking for a house in London without a map.
> 2 Grouping plant species into a hierarchy of bigger and bigger groups makes identifying plants much easier. We must be able to identify plants quickly and accurately if we are to identify those parts of the world's vegetation that contain the greatest diversity of plants ... these areas are at the top of the list of conservation priorities.
> 3 Understanding how plants have evolved in the past may help us to predict how they will evolve in the future as climate changes.'

The difference between this and the application of taxonomy to managing knowledge and information in organizations lies in the fact that the families to which plants belong can be verified, for example by DNA; whereas the way we group ideas about the main business of an organization and classify its collections of information is a matter of human choice, related to values.[1]

Nevertheless the botanists' reasoning can be applied to knowledge and information management. Organizational taxonomy can:
1 Help to point us to likeliest places for finding what we need

---

1 Human choice and values in fact are an essential part of the classifications of science too; as Gould (2002, pp289–90) puts it: 'We can best defend the scientific vitality of taxonomy by asserting ... that all systems of classification must express theories about the causes of order, and must therefore feature a complex mixture of concepts and percepts – that is, preferences in human thinking combined with observations of nature's often cryptic realities.'

Unpacking taxonomy

In the portmanteau:

Tools of the mind (traditional)

- Group things with common features, according to what's important to us

- Label them to help us:
  Put them away in store
  Find them whenever we need them

- Provide standards for grouping and labelling.

Technology tools (modern)

- Help people in using their knowledge, to create tools of the mind

- Make it easy for them to use the tools to manage what they know

- Reduce intellectual and economic cost of doing the job

- Provide 'invisible help'.

Figure 7.2
Unpacking taxonomy

2 Help us put new information in the appropriate context, relate it to things it belongs with, and so get early value from it, and know what to keep
3 Help us predict the future from looking at the past – by giving access to organizational memory.

The basis of this approach to making sense of information lies in the way human minds work. What McArthur (1986, pp32–3) calls 'the taxonomic urge', to group things and ideas according to what's important and/or valuable for us, seems to be built into the human mind. The business of making connections and seeing relations among things is the basis of our learning from childhood on, and this natural predisposition has led us to create the tools of the mind and the supporting technological tools shown in Figure 7.2 (*see* above). The traditional tools of the mind went seriously out of fashion for a period when full-text searching of large databases developed, and than had to be 'rediscovered' when internet search engines proved not quite up to the job; as Edols (2001) puts it: 'Major corporate Intranets and portals are now involved in the restructuring of their sites so that effective information management and retrieval is a priority. This almost always involves the use of concepts based on cataloguing principles such as classification, indexing and controlled vocabularies. ... users must be able to find the information they want quickly and easily which is not always possible when relying on full text searching or browsing through unstructured links.'

Just as grouping objects and ideas is a fundamental human activity, so too is giving them names, so that we can communicate with one another about them. Unfortunately we're not very good at being consistent in our naming; we don't always agree with one another about what to call things, and it is even difficult to be consistent with ourselves – we call the same thing by different names at different times. And while that adds a pleasing linguistic variety, it can make it difficult to find information if similar things are stored under different names, and different things under the same name.

The taxonomy tools of the mind are designed to take advantage of the human tendencies to group and name, and to overcome our inconsistencies in doing it, by helping us to set *standards* for:

1 Grouping our ideas about whatever we need to know about (*classifications*)
2 Providing pointers to the actual content of items and collections of items (*indexes*)
3 Naming the subjects and objects that make up the information content we need to maintain our knowledge (*thesauri*)
4 Labelling the different kinds of 'containers' into which we put the information (*metadata*).

> *Classifications* work from the top down; they involve grouping together related concepts according to some common feature into classes and hierarchies; items added to a classified collection are assigned to a place in it according to rules established as part of the classification. This tool was developed intensively in the 19th and 20th centuries, for arranging libraries.

> *Indexes* are developed 'from the bottom up'. They provide pointers to the actual content of items and collections of items; they were originally arranged in alpha order, as book indexes still are. They are valuable because they can complement classifications, compensating for the fact that whatever principle of grouping we choose for classifying, it will separate some things with similar features in the process of bringing others together. Indexes help users to find items relevant to what they need, whatever classification category or collection they have been assigned to. It is impossible to over-estimate their importance as devices which allow freedom of movement into records that represent things, and flexibility in manipulating them in order to get the information we need.

> *Thesauri* embody standards for the use of terms; they are a means of bringing the terms used to describe items of information under control by providing consistent terms for indexing information, and guidance in searching for it.

> The essential elements of any thesaurus are:

1 Index terms
The standard terms which it is decided to use for indexing the information put into a system

2 Entry terms
Alternatives to the standard terms, which it is decided not to use for indexing, but which have to be listed in the thesaurus, so that users of the thesaurus are guided from them to the standard terms

3 Instructions
To help people who index information, and those who search for it, by:
* Pointing the way from entry terms to index terms * Linking specific index terms with broader ones in the same subject field * Relating index terms to other relevant ones.

4 Guidance on the use of terms
* Definitions of terms * Advice on when to use them.

Thesauri are arranged in various ways; often with both alphabetical and classified structures.

Metadata are standard descriptive 'labels' for the 'containers' of information, supplementing what index terms and classification groups provide; they show such details as authorship, date, place of origin, level of confidentiality, intended audience, type of document, etc.

These tools are laborious to create using traditional means (as I can testify from experience of compiling indexes and constructing thesauri 'by hand' using no more sophisticated technology than a manual typewriter and index cards), and they impose high intellectual and economic costs on both makers and users of the manual versions. So from quite an early stage in the use of computers technological tools were devised to help the process. Today's technological tools provide powerful invisible help, which reduces the intellectual costs and gives long-established tools of the mind new power. The most sophisticated are designed to help people in an organization to:
* Categorize the content of its information resources * Build a taxonomy and classification based on its business * Create an indexing terminology based on the words it uses.

They *can* do it automatically, but only crudely; they need human intervention to get a solution that matches the organization's needs, and human knowledge to provide a 'supervised learning system' for the software. The best of them are based on the principle that it is unsound to rely wholly on either humans or algorithms (*see* Clarke, 2001, for a clear description of what one of them – Verity – can do).

The great service that taxonomy tools can do for organizations is to give them a 'common currency' for managing the knowledge and information they need for success. Table 7.1, (*see* next page) sets out what organizations need to do, and why they can't do it without this 'common currency'.

Without the common currency that taxonomy tools can give, organizations risk:
* Missing what they need to know * Taking the wrong action as a result
* Endangering their ability to survive and prosper * Not learning from experience,

What organizations need to do	Why they need a common currency to do it
Keep their knowledge fed with the right information so that they can act effectively	They can't do it unless they define and collect the right information; and group and label it so that it can be found
Collect the right information to feed their knowledge	They can't do it without standards for grouping, naming and labelling what they collect
Manage the information they are responsible for, so that it's accessible to everyone whenever it's needed	They can't do it without standards for grouping, naming and labelling what they manage
Exchange knowledge and information productively with the outside world and inside the organization	They can't do it without a common language for exchanges, so that people understand one another
Access the results of their actions and learn from them	They can't do that effectively without standards for recording the outcomes of action
Make economic use of information resources; minimize searching time; maximize results of searching	They can't do that without 'keys' for getting and searching them effectively

Table 7.1
Why organizations need a 'common currency'

repeating costly mistakes ● Working unproductively and uneconomically ● Not making the contacts they need.

This section has emphasized thinking human beings as the initiators in interaction between 'tools of the mind' and tools of technology.

The relevant lessons for information strategy development: ● Keep the organization's definitions of essential knowledge and information in line with what it seeks to do ● Ensure that it has appropriate 'tools of the mind' for setting and maintaining standards, and that people are able to use them, with full support from the technology.

And a quotation from a great scientist, the late Stephen J Gould, to round off this taxonomic discussion:

'The impediments of outmoded systems may sow frustration and discord, but if we force our minds to search for more fruitful arrangements and to challenge our propensity for passive acceptance of traditional thinking, then we may expand the realms of conceptual space by the most apparently humble, yet most markedly effective, intellectual device: the development of a new taxonomic scheme to break a mental logjam.' (Gould, 2002)

Now, to complete our consideration of why organizations need to integrate information, technology, and human interactions, we need to look at how humans in organizations interact with one another and with IT.

Organizations consist of human beings – and how to make the best of it

The most important thing I've learned from many years as an 'organization-fancier' is this:

Everything that happens in organizations depends on human minds, human feelings, and human action, and the owners of the minds and feelings have their own axes to grind and fish to fry; they don't leave their individual and group values, their conflicting interests, their personal agendas, or their eccentricities and cussedness, on the doorstep when they enter their place of work – they bring them right inside with them. And getting the best rather than the worst for the organization out of that requires low-cost but long-term investment – mainly of thinking time.

Yet today we see the paradox of businesses which are beginning to grasp the need to 'manage knowledge' – but which at the same time impose pressures and compulsions under the threat of competition, take inadequate time for reflection, and depend more and more on complex IT, without paying enough attention to how people need to interact with the technology and with one another in the pursuit of all the electronically mediated transactions they aspire to.

Knowledge and information will not be used unless humans are willing to use them; IT will do nothing for organizations without human decisions and interactions between humans and systems, and between people. That is the only condition on which the technology will help us to use our minds and feelings more creatively and constructively, and to act more effectively. And the most important help the technology can give is in making it rewarding and easy to transform knowledge to information and information to knowledge, to exchange knowledge, and to find information.

So how should organizations manage human/technology and human/human relations, so as to support free people in exercising their knowledge to benefit themselves, their colleagues, their organization, and the 'outside world' on which it depends for its livelihood? (I say 'free people' because knowledge-based work requires 'volunteers' who take the responsibility for thinking for themselves, rather than 'conscripts' who carry out routine procedures.)

They could make a start by recognizing that humans, individually and collectively, can and do exist without IT. They've been organizing themselves pretty well since prehistoric times, just by talking to each other.

And technology isn't always involved in the greatest advances. Sometimes it is – the revolution that Galileo brought in our understanding of the universe depended on the technology he himself did so much to develop; but the equally revolutionary changes that Darwin achieved owed little if anything to technology and most to observation based on, as he put it, 'some ideas' and long reflection.

It is particularly instructive to read about brilliant human/technology co-operation in using information during the Second World War, when survival depended on it, and the earliest computers were just on the horizon.

 Checkland and Holwell (1998, Chapter 5) tell the enthralling story of the Battle of Britain information system. Incoming information from a variety of low-tech and non-tech sources went through a 'filter room' before going to the operations room – the job of the highly experienced people there was to assess the quality of the information flowing in, on the basis of their knowledge of individual radar stations and operators, and to make rapid judgements and sort out discrepancies to upgrade it before passing it on. The filter room was characteristic of the development of new information roles, which used experience and combined skills in new ways.

The code-breaking centre at Bletchley Park ('Station X') started with a similar combination of knowledgeable motivated people and the then available communications technology. By good fortune, one of the people was a genius: Alan Turing, who developed the first practical computer application, to support human intellectual power in code breaking, at a critical time in the war. Apart from that first revolutionary piece of IT, the successful solution was, like the Battle of Britain one, an information system that used human intelligence and existing technology in the right combination. And just as Fighter Command had its filter room, Bletchley Park instituted a new information-assessing role – the key job of Fusion Officer. The job consisted, uniquely for a system which had to rely for security on there being no communication among different groups of information workers, of bringing together information from different areas, assessing possible connections and interpretations, and bringing the results to the key decision makers.

Those stories are a vivid illustration of the simple and self-evident fact that the only agency that can turn information into knowledge and act constructively on it is the human mind, embodied in human beings with all their rich and odd variety – and that is something that can't be replaced by IT. People, as Itami (1987) reminded us a good while ago, are the embodiment of 'invisible assets' who 'carry and exchange the information necessary for strategic fit'.

And Davenport & Prusak (1998) pointed out more recently that knowledge creation 'remains largely an act of individuals or groups and their brains.' It is indeed liberating to recognize that organizations are not wholly and always the rational enterprises they like to present themselves to be. To insist on assuming that they are, is really flying in the face of common sense, and a demonstration of naive idealism – and it misses the chance of profiting from the creativity that goes along with the human oddities. It is also naive to be so dominated by using the products of technology as to forget that they represent just one aspect of human activity, and one way of looking at the world. If we lose faith in our own power of thinking and acting on our thoughts, we can fall victim to the fragility of complex IT systems and compound the consequences of their breakdowns (*see* Collins, 1997, for examples).

What information systems should do for us

To finish this discussion of the proper and productive co-operation between humans and systems, here is a summary of what systems should do to support people in making good use of information: • Store information neatly and elegantly • Help users to get back to it whenever it is relevant • Help them to reach people who know about things they need to understand, and to converse with them • Retain the results of experience (failure as well as success) in such a way that the organization can learn from them • Help people to interchange information and ideas informally • Capture the essentials from informal exchanges for long-term use • Scan all information resources as if they were one • Help people to keep track of significant change in the outside world and within the organization • Remind them to do things in time • Remind them of those to whom they should communicate informa-

Information strategy in practice

tion • Present information in acceptable and helpful formats for what the users need to do with it • Do routine things effectively and efficiently, without making users jump through hoops.

If systems make it easy to get at information managed by a different department, tell colleagues what we are doing, ask them for help or advice, we are more likely to get into the habit of using them in those ways. So when new systems are being planned, the planning should take account of the information interchanges – within the organization and with its 'outside world' – which people need to make in order to do their job properly.

Interactions among human beings need human-centred support

That brings us to the interactions which need to take place between human beings for information and knowledge to be properly used in organizations. Over the last few years, in working on auditing courses with information professionals who face the prospect of managing audits in their organizations, it has become evident that they generally perceive organizational culture, and the interactions it promotes or inhibits, as a major obstacle to achieving anything useful from the process, and that they are deeply concerned to find ways of dealing with it (*see* Orna, 2000b). And in working with organizations on recent information audits, and seeing how people in them express their experiences in trying to get and use information (*see* the description of the workshops, pp40–44, 69–72). I have been made aware of their perceptions of:
• The impermeable layer between the celestial regions where TOTO (the top of the organization) lives and the rest of the organization • The disparity between the kinds of information that TOTO is thought to value, and that which individuals most value for their own work • The differing cultures of organizational 'tribes' – especially in organizations formed from mergers, and in those with a central head office and outlying regions • The 'silos' that dot the organizational landscape, their contents inaccessible to all but their owners • The ignorance of other people's work, and of the connections and potential information flows between different jobs, that prevails even within departments • The weakness, or total lack, of essential information interchanges between the organization and people it depends on in its out-side world.

All those shortcomings threaten the success of the multitude of technologically based initiatives – from e-government to extranets, e-commerce to information architectures – which organizations are currently pursuing; yet investment in overcoming them is minimal compared with investment in the technology, which is perceived as primary. Hyams (2002) describes a serious attempt to put this situation right in the UK Department of Trade and Industry. Liz Maclachlan, the senior information manager responsible for developing the DTI's new information architecture and electronic document and records management programme, insists that the main effort has to lie in instilling a different attitude to managing information throughout all staff: 'Like many organizations we have invested heavily in IT, such as our intranet, but have been disappointed with the return. We did not give enough attention at the start to agreeing standards and conventions about how we would work together – for example in email best practice ... And we trained people in how to use the systems, but not in how to manage the information on them. The result is that in many cases people have developed their own systems and techniques. These personal systems are often inaccessible to others, and can be lost when somebody moves on.'

Recent research at Loughborough University about the attributes of information as an asset, and its role in enhancing organizational effectiveness, produced similar findings (Oppenheim, Stenson, & Wilson, 2002). The senior managers they interviewed clearly recognized the role of people in information and knowledge management initiatives but 'little investment was directed here. Encouraging sharing and collaborative cultures, reusing information and implementing successful intranets were all seen to be people-centric activities but the methods used to implement these were almost exclusively technical.' The researchers' diagnosis is that: 'Senior managers who are measured and managed according to strict performance criteria have little scope to implement more people-centred initiatives which promote knowledge-sharing. Senior managers may require training and more wide ranging inclusive performance criteria if they are to gain the benefits of information assets in their organizations.'

They point to a possible solution through the idea of 'social capital', defined by Cohen and Prusak (2001, p4) as 'the stock of active connections between people: the trust, mutual understanding, and shared values and behaviors that bind the members of human networks and communities and make co-operative action possible.'

I have started to recommend to organizations one practical action towards encouraging the kind of mutual understanding and productive negotiation over information discussed here. It is an application of what Marchand et al (2001, p277) call the 'principle of reciprocal information responsibility'. Organizations can help themselves greatly, at comparatively little cost, if they:

● Map the exchanges of information and knowledge that are needed among job holders to achieve what the organization is in business for ● Build into all job descriptions the mutual information obligations that go with the job; the people to whom job holders owe information, and those who owe them information; the groups inside and out with whom they should exchange knowledge ● Provide training and support for this aspect of the job ● Include it in performance appraisal ● Make sure that the IT/systems infrastructure supports people in making the essential exchanges.

Essex County Council have recently taken an innovative step which could help to put these principles into effect, and to bridge the gap between 'people-centric' aims and technology-centred action described above. They identified a missing link in their management of information: between 'information sharing' on the one hand and meeting legal and data security requirements on the other.

This commonsense recognition of the fact that it's no good telling people to share information, if you don't also tell them *what* they ought to share and *with whom*, and under what conditions, and what must remain confidential, led to the creation of the new post of Corporate Information Sharing and Information Security (ISIS) Manager.

The purpose of the job is to develop and implement 'an effective corporate strategy, policies and procedures for sharing information legally and securely'.

The ISIS Manager is accountable for:

● Conforming to the requirements of Freedom of Information Act, 2000, Data Protection Act, 1998, and other relevant legislation ● Working with other organizations to prepare a Trust Charter for Electronic Service Delivery, Codes of Practice and

Protocols for information sharing between the Council, its partner agencies and Essex citizens, including, but not limited to, Electronic Service Delivery ● Co-ordinating, undertaking, maintaining and regularly reviewing a complete audit of information and knowledge assets, and preparing a Publication Scheme to meet the requirements of Data Protection and Freedom of Information legislation ● Raising awareness of the legal and technical implications of ISIS policies and procedures.

The relevant lessons for information strategy development:

> **Lesson**
>
> ● Balance investment in technology with appropriate investment in supporting human interactions ● Value human minds and reward thinking I Support and reward reciprocal information responsibility.

Section 2
The real value organizations get from information

This is a knotty but critical subject, with which I have battled for several years (*see* Orna, 1996, 1999); so have a lot of other people whose judgement I respect; there are good reasons, which are summed up in these two quotations:

> 'The whole area of information and knowledge management, their role in value creation and impact on business performance seem to be fraught with difficulty for the organisations we studied.' (Oppenheim et al 2002).

> '… if one cannot measure the impact of IT on economic productivity or the role of information use in business organizations, then discussions of the "knowledge economy" or "information-based organizations" are interesting, but not compelling.' (Marchand et al 2002, p248).

In other words, the ideas can be hard for the people who control the money to grasp, and even when they do understand them, if we can't show them a good convincing link between using information well and business success, they aren't going to part with the money for managing information.

So I would be failing the readers of this book if I didn't try to explain what I think are the essential ideas about what makes information and knowledge valuable to organizations, and to summarize the findings of recent sound research which seem to point to a solution to the problem that has beset all who manage information for many years.

The peculiarities of information and knowledge resources

To start with, a summary of how information and knowledge differ from material resources when it comes to value:

1 Information, on the definition used in this book (*see* p7) has no inbuilt value; it acquires value only when human minds have transformed it into knowledge (*see* p8), without which no products of tangible value can be created or exchanged.
2 If information and knowledge are exchanged and traded, the value from using them can increase for all parties to the transaction.
3 The potential value of information is not reduced by use; it can be transformed

into knowledge and used many times by many users to add value to many activities and outputs. As Itami and Roehl (1987) put it, 'The essence of invisible assets is information, and it is this characteristic, which is not shared by other resources, that makes a free ride possible. Only information-based assets can be used in multiple ways at the same time ...' And information 'can be used simultaneously, it does not wear out from over use, and bits of it can be combined to yield even more information.'

4 Information doesn't just sit around in 'information repositories' which constitute 'information assets'; it also, and more significantly, enters into all business activities of all organizations – it is a diffused resource.

Those characteristics of information and knowledge point to the essential fact that their value for organizations (which may be positive or negative) comes from people transforming information into knowledge and acting on the knowledge to do something. This is why concentrating on 'intellectual capital' and 'information assets', popular in the 1990s, hasn't got anywhere much. There's not much hope of getting a nice tidy 'bottom line' value for them because:

● Assets are static, but knowledge and information are dynamic ● The only 'assets' you can see and count are 'containers' of information ● That misses their content, and, worse, how people use information content – which enters into all transactions and processes; and worse still, it misses the effects of using it and what they imply for the future ● Using information content means transforming it into knowledge and acting on it ● And it's only from the effects of that process that you can judge the value that information adds to or subtracts from other assets.

(That is why information auditing is a useful approach. It won't give you a financial value for information assets, but what it tells you about how people in the organization use information and knowledge will give pointers to:

● Where processes are adding or subtracting value ● Changes that could move value towards the positive end of the scale ● How to evaluate the effects of using information and knowledge as you go, so that the organization can assess future value and make sound strategic decisions.)

Valuing information and knowledge is not an objective exercise

The other important fact to remember is that no valuing of anything, including information, can take place without human judgement about the relative value of different things in relation to what the people doing the judging want to achieve. Of course human judgement can't be anything but 'subjective' – but organizations hire people, particularly for 'knowledge work' and for high-level management posts, precisely for their ability and experience in exercising professional judgement on their behalf. So what's the objection to applying that kind of judgement to the value of the knowledge and information they need to use in their work?

Both the Loughborough research, and the large-scale project described by Marchand et al in their two books about it (2001, 2002) take this line of reasoning, and make short work of the objection to 'non-objective' methods of ascertaining the business value of knowledge and information. The Loughborough researchers concluded:

'To put it bluntly, arriving at a value of information or knowledge is not an objective exercise. Different stakeholders (customers, employees, managers, owners and investors) will employ different methods depending on their various perspectives. Their evaluations will be subjective. Attempts to value information and place it on the balance sheet of organizations does have benefits in that it positions information within an area of financial management with which all senior managers are concerned. However, an objective value of information is not possible in our view. Information value by its very nature is subjective, dependent on the interpretation of the individual or team members who employ information in particular situations for particular purposes. Objective measures are also often far less reliable than they at first appear. Recently, accounting has been highlighted as an area where organisations can present seemingly objective and audited financial statements, eg, Enron, which have in fact little to do with their real underlying financial position.' (Oppenheim et al 2002a)

And they state plainly in the final report on the research that:

'Attempting to place a value on information which was dynamic and subject to the changing perceptions of users was seen as an impossible task.... Almost all of the senior managers interviewed saw a role for information assets in enhancing the effectiveness of their organisations. They also saw a role for information assets in improving communication and decision-making in their organisations. However, the practical application of information assets to these issues may be more dependent on how people use and apply information in everyday situations. ... there is a link, tentative as it may be, between information assets and organisational effectiveness. Any organisation which is concerned with achieving effectiveness must also be concerned with the management of its information assets ...The leveraging of information assets requires more than technological solutions. It also requires attention to the long-term building of assets for future economic benefit.' (Oppenheim et al 2002b)

The link between information orientation and business performance

Those conclusions, from a small though thoroughly researched sample of UK organizations and their managers, receive strong support from the work of Marchand and his colleagues (2001, 2002) with a large international sample of senior managers in a variety of businesses (their findings have already been referred to in Chapter 6.2, pp113–115). They present a method for measuring the link between mature 'information orientation' and good business performance. When they began their research, it appeared that '...there has been no significant progress, until now, for establishing a practical business metric of effective information use that was causally linked to business performance improvement.' (op cit, p248). As it proceeded, they found both good and bad news; the 'good news' was:

'... that managers in many companies have learned how to integrate people, information and IT to achieve superior business performance.'

the bad:

'that they have had no clear metric for evaluating the interactive effects of people, information, and IT on business performance in their business units or companies.' Marchand et al (2002), p148

The researchers set about trying to develop such a metric. They first looked for an 'objective' measure that would be valid across the different countries and different types of business in their sample, but found difficulties in the way, in particular the wide variations in reporting requirements on performance of companies in different countries, and the differences between what privately and publicly held firms divulge about performance. They concluded that '... the additional use of "objective" measures of performance was not possible nor advisable, given these quality constraints.' So, they chose instead to use qualitative, but statistically reliable, methods, depending on the evaluation of knowledgeable people in the population they were looking at. They decided to use 'a perceived multi-indicator of business performance that has been considered superior in previous management research under these circumstances, rather than "objective" or secondary measures.'

The indicator was senior managers' perceptions of their own company's business performance (a 'subjective' judgement, but one likely to be pretty accurate), as given by their answers to these questions:

> 'Relative to our competitors:
> 1 Our market share growth has been ...
> 2 Our financial performance has been ...
> 3 Our level of product and service innovation has been ...
> 4 Our ability to achieve a superior company reputation has been ...'
> (op cit p147)

Their final conclusion was that 'effective information use does lead to better business performance but the link is through I[nformation] O[rientation]' that is, through *combining* effective management of information, IT, and organizational behaviour in relation to information and knowledge; IO 'predicts business performance much more powerfully than the three capabilities independently.' (op cit p149). They also concluded that people are fundamental to getting better business performance via Information Orientation, because:

> 'organizations involve relationships among people, and how people choose to contribute their knowledge to achieve organizational purposes. People are constantly balancing their own interests against the group and organization's interests, in deciding whether and how to contribute their personal expertise, skills, and experience to the welfare of the group or organization. The organization defines a relevant context to continuously convert human knowledge and learning into creative ideas and innovations of value to achieving organizational success in the future, rather than for today alone.' (op cit p150)

These are important current ideas about the solid value of information for business performance that information professionals in particular need to understand and to be able to explain.

Looking both back and forward

So if we want to get an idea of what kinds of information and knowledge are going to have future business value, we have to look both back and forward – back at the results of using them in all contexts of organization's work, and forward at what that teaches us for their likely future impact on performance. And we can't do that without taking the experiences of people in using information and knowledge, and their value judgements about them, into account.

And if, as Marchand and his colleagues observe, 'Senior managers have developed a good feel for success, but find it difficult to say precisely what decisions or actions actually led to their success ...' (op cit, p249), then it's for information professionals to develop and demonstrate the means of identifying what the use of information and knowledge contributes to success.

The lessons for information strategy are that it should:

Lesson

* Monitor how people use information and knowledge in the organization's work
* Record the results of initiatives and make them accessible ● Collect examples of value added by information orientation, of risks from which it has saved the organization, and of failures and errors that could have been avoided by better use of information.

That kind of strategy means relating the use of knowledge and information to:
* Changes: in the organization's 'outside world' and its inner world ● Its response to changes initiated by others ● Changes that it seeks to initiate.

So the next section is about ...

Section 3
Applying knowledge and information to meet and initiate change

' ... the dynamics of knowledge impose one clear imperative: every organization has to build the management of change into its very structure. [And they have] to do something, and not say "Let's make another study".'
Drucker (1995, pp70–71)

Change is indeed interwoven in all life, inseparable from the world we live in, an essential part of what makes us human; and it was by seeking to understand and control change, that the human intellect in which we take such pride evolved. So organizations and individuals fly in the face of nature when they try to remain unchanging. No organization is ever static, and the way in which they change over time is in fact one of the factors from which we can learn most.

As to the other point that Drucker makes – the necessity of doing something when you think there is a change to be made, we should remember the words of Checkland and Scholes (1990/1999, p52): changes have to be both 'systematically desirable' and 'culturally feasible' if they are to be successfully acted on. That means that not only should the organization recognize the account of the situation presented[2] as being relevant to the problem under consideration, and the changes proposed as desirable; the changes must also be 'perceived as meaningful within [the organization's] culture, within its worldview.' You have to 'think not only about the substance of the intended change itself but also about the additional things you normally have to do in human situations to enable change to occur' (op cit, pA29) – and those things usually take a long time (*see* the stories at the start of this chapter).

2 The authors are referring to uses of soft systems methodology, but what they say is also applicable to the results of information auditing.

Four kinds of change

I find it helpful in thinking about organizations and change to sub-divide change into four possible kinds, as shown in Figure 7.3 opposite, according to whether it is expected or unexpected, and whether it originates outside the organization or within it. At least that moves us away from the unfortunately prevalent view that change is always something (usually nasty) that is done to us. (For examples of typical changes of the four kinds, and of what organizations need to know to manage them successfully, *see* Orna, 1999, pp154–159)

Applying knowledge and information to change

Organizations need to be equipped, through an appropriate combination of human knowledge, skills, and technology:
1 To protect themselves against being 'ambushed' by changes
2 To spot significant changes on the horizon in good time to be able to plan how to turn them to advantage
3 To seize opportunities for initiating changes advantageous to themselves.
   The exercise of the required skills (which are a typical part of the good information professional's armoury) is described by Marchand and his colleagues (2002, pp78–79) as 'sensing' – continuously identifying events, trends and changes in external business conditions, and making sense out of them, so as to define the organizational information needs implicit in them . Organizations need

> '…perceptual skills to recognize changes in the competitive environment and knowing which business stimuli are relevant to an individual's business context. If these skills and judgements are weak, then new information requirements are not completely anticipated and new sources of information ill defined. … It is through sensing that a company's members and managers observe: (1) changes between their current perceptions and associated ways of collecting and using information inside a company; and (2) changes in business conditions that require a reinterpretation of threats, opportunities, risks, as well as the ways information is collected and used. We can distinguish companies by how well organizational members sense changes in business conditions and respond to them.' (op cit, p79)

Those are valuable lessons on the first two points listed above. For the third – seizing opportunities for initiating changes – organizations also need to create new knowledge and apply it. To quote from what I wrote in an earlier book (Orna 1999, p160).

> 'The highest and most productive level in the strategic use of information and knowledge – as such Japanese writers as Itami (1987) and Nonaka and Takeuchi (1995) have demonstrated – lies in creating new knowledge, which can then be applied to get the best out of change, in both responding and initiating modes. Itami and his American co-author Roehl distinguish various levels of 'fit' between the organization's strategy for using what it knows, and the environment in which it operates. At the level of 'active fit' organizations 'can sometimes change the environment by a judicious choice of strategy or can at least anticipate external changes'. A higher level is the so-called 'leveraged fit' between the organization and its environment. Here the organization 'does more than anticipate and res-

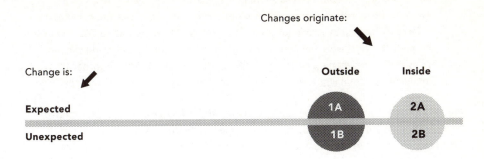

The cells of the matrix:

1A
Expected change originating in the outside world

Examples:
- New legislation
- Demographic and social change in the population the organization serves
- Changes in manufacturing technology/ materials

1B
Unexpected change originating in the outside world

Examples:
- Natural disaster affecting the supply/ price of raw materials
- Premises destroyed by terrorist bomb
- Hostile takeover bid
- Competing products launched which undermine the market

2A
Expected change originating within the organization

Examples:
- Flotation of the company on the stock market
- A decision to move to a 'partnership' type of organization, with a commitment to acknowledging the organization's responsibilities to all who are involved in its activities or affected by them
- A decision to outsource IT

2B
Unexpected change originating within the organization

Examples:
- A decision by the owners to close a plant, announced without warning to its management and staff
- Losses caused by a rogue trader or dishonest manager
- High staff turnover or absenteeism caused by imposed changes in working practices

Figure 7.3
Matrix of four kinds of change

pond to future changes in the environment; it uses those very environmental characteristics that are seen as limiting at the passive and active levels of strategic fit to make its strategy more effective' – that is, it uses the constraints it faces as the stimulus to innovation. An example: the clockwork radio and more recently the clockwork personal computer; the constraint of lack of power supplies in rural developing countries has been the stimulus to their inventor to innovate by combining a twentieth century technology with a medieval one.'

Figure 7.4 suggests the way in which knowledge and information can help to move organizations from spending most of their time responding to unexpected change towards a situation of 'change mastery' where they use foresight and insight to initiate change.

The lessons for information strategy in relation to change are:

Lesson

• Give thinking time to understanding the organization's own culture, and to working out strategies for feasible changes • Provide resources of finance and skill for environmental sensing, for bringing the results of it into organizational consciousness and knowledge, and for managing the relevant information content • Recognize the need for both information management and knowledge management (the subject of the next and final section of this chapter).

Section 4
How KM and IM are related, and why we need both

Knowledge management is potentially of great value, but in danger of not fulfilling its potential for organizations. One of the main reasons is confusion about what knowledge management and information management consist of, and the relationship between them (for the definitions used in this book, *see* pp9–10). At worst, it's assumed that once you have a post labelled something like 'Chief Knowledge Officer' and the technology to go with it, information management and the lowly people who engage are no longer required; if something called information management does actually continue to exist, no connection is perceived between it and the high-status activity called knowledge management.

The organization where the information audit described in the part 2 of Chapter 3 and part 2 of Chapter 4 was carried out was far from being such a worst case, but the audit showed that it did have some problems about the relation between KM and IM. It had established a knowledge management team of well qualified information professionals, and aimed to develop a knowledge management strategy – the information audit was indeed planned as a step towards that.The report on the audit summed up the problems:

• 'The role and responsibilities of the Knowledge Management team appear as yet not to be well understood within the organization • Although today it is accepted by leaders in good practice in KM that the knowledge which individuals need to use in their work cannot be maintained and managed successfully without the support of properly managed resources of information, this level of information management is not at present provided for in the organization. The KM team themselves are well aware of this, and wish to remedy the deficiency

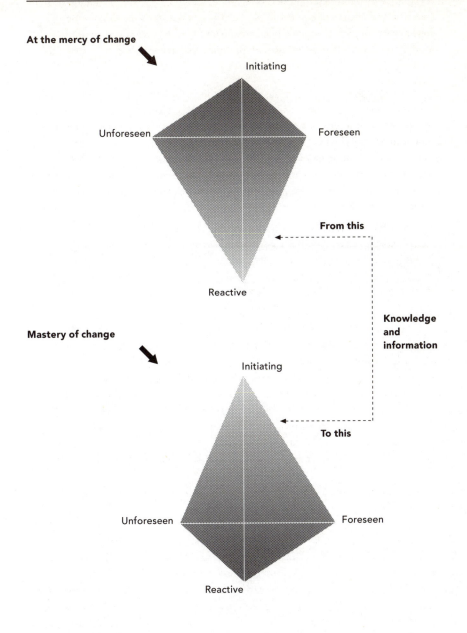

Figure 7.4
From being at the mercy of change to mastery of change

● High-quality information professionals are employed, but they currently do not have the opportunity of exercising their professional skills to the organization's full advantage. Lack of support in managing information is a key cause for the kind of problems reported by every department and every individual contributing to the audit.'

And it recommended, to improve the situation:

'That the organization build on its existing strengths in knowledge management and on initiatives already taken by the KM team, to develop integrated know-ledge and information management by a group drawing on appropriate existing specialisms within the organization (including knowledge and information manage-ment, systems/IT, human resources, communications), headed by a manager at an appropriate level.

Responsibilities of the group: developing, co-ordinating and managing the unified knowledge and information repository; developing and implementing policy in this area; contributing to the development of the organization's business strat-egies, supporting staff who manage specific information resources.'

The arguments for integrated KM and IM

These are the main arguments for why organizations need integrated management of both knowledge and information:

What makes human beings unique is our ability to structure and manage what we know in our heads, to transform and communicate it to others, and to use it as the basis for action to achieve goals – in the course of which we create new knowl-edge. Knowledge lives only in human minds; it can exist only if there is a human mind to do the knowing. From that it follows that:

A The individual humans who have knowledge in their minds are the first people who have to manage it

B Therefore organizational knowledge management means managing so as to sup-port people so that they can use what they know effectively

and

C That kind of support cannot be given unless information is managed strategically.

The foundation for managing this rich combination of people, their knowledge and the information necessary to keep their knowledge in good health needs to be a strong one – not least because, as noted earlier in this chapter, the human minds that create knowledge and keep it alive come 'bundled' with human nature. Establishing it usually means seeking to change at least some aspects of organizational culture, and that process cannot be an instant, or even a rapid, one (though it is not a hope-less task, for real-life examples of actions taken by managers to bring about 'cultural' change as expressed in information behaviours that bring reward and reinforcement, *see* Marchand et al 2001, Chapter 4).

It is certainly not possible to establish what is usually referred to as 'knowledge sharing' through incorporating it in mission or vision statements. The term has always seemed to me an amazingly vague and optimistic one, especially in the mouths of managers dedicated to hard-headed competition; there is about as much hope of selling it in the average organization as there is of persuading a roomful of three-year-olds that it's nice to share toys. Informed and honest negotiation, in the framework of what Davenport and Prusak (1998, Chapter 2) call the organizational 'knowledge market', seems much more realistic and attainable.

Knowledge management implies a foundation of accepted obligations, rights, and principles within the organization.

Knowledge obligations

The organization's obligations towards the people who work in it are to:
* Respect knowledge in the minds of people as their own permanent property
* Organize work so that people spend the largest possible amount of their working time using their knowledge at the highest level * Provide support, education and training to enable those who work in the organization to meet their knowledge obligations.

And the reciprocal obligations of those who work in the organization are to:
* Be aware of what they need to know to do their job and of the information needs of those with whom they interact in their work * Use information to keep their knowledge fit to support their work * Interchange information and knowledge with colleagues and people outside the organization to help it achieve its aims
* Manage conscientiously the resources of information for which they are responsible * Make their knowledge available to the organization by transforming it into information and contributing it to the organization's information resources.

Knowledge principles

Organizations should commit themselves to:
1 Defining
* The knowledge they need to achieve their goals * The information they need to maintain it * How they need to use knowledge and information
2 Keeping the definitions up to date as their goals develop and change
3 Auditing their use of knowledge and information regularly
4 Ensuring that they acquire and create the information they need to support their knowledge, and manage it effectively
5 Providing for a co-ordinated overview of their total resources of knowledge and information
6 Maintaining an infrastructure of systems and IT to support management of information resources, and interactions among people in using knowledge
7 Using knowledge and information ethically in all their internal and external dealings, to preserve and enhance their reputation.

The domains of KM and IM

The domains of KM and IM are, as Figure 7.5 (*see* p143) shows, distinct, but mutually dependent, and there is a significant area where they overlap.

The domain of knowledge management covers:
* The transformations of knowledge to information and information to knowledge that only human minds can make * Support for people in organizations in managing them * Minimizing the intellectual and financial costs to individuals and orga-

nizations of transforming knowledge to information and contributing it to the organization's information resources ⊛ Maximizing the resulting gains ⊛ Promoting knowledge exchange in a 'market' where transactions are sanctioned and safeguarded, and can take place under conditions of mutual trust ⊛ Negotiating limits to what knowledge can and cannot be exchanged inside the organization and between it and its outside world ⊛ Helping individuals and the organization to define and keep their knowledge obligations ⊛ Promoting organizational learning.

The domain of information management lies in:

⊛ Acquiring, storing, making accessible information to maintain organizational knowledge in appropriate information resources ⊛ Co-ordinating the information resources that support knowledge and to which people contribute their knowledge ⊛ Providing new information resources to meet changes in the environment ⊛ Managing the information emerging from knowledge markets ⊛ Using information systems and IT appropriately and innovatively to support knowledge exchange, interactions and negotiations, and the finding, diffusion and communication of information ⊛ Making the lessons of experience accessible as an information resource for individual and organizational learning.

The territory that the two share consists of:

⊛ The knowledge and information implications of what the organization thinks it's in business for ⊛ Policy and strategy for using knowledge and information to support business processes ⊛ The value added by using knowledge and information ⊛ Monitoring change ('sensing' as Marchand and his colleagues call it) in external and internal environments for potential effects on what knowledge and in formation the organization needs to create its offerings and achieve its objectives ⊛ Monitoring and evaluating the effects of using knowledge and information ⊛ Bringing the results of monitoring into central strategic decision making ⊛ Matching the way knowledge and information are managed to the direction in which organization seeks to go, to its existing culture(s), and to desired cultural changes.

What integrated KM and IM can bring

When I go into organizations and learn about the experience of the staff who work there, I often find myself resenting on their behalf the obstacles that thwart the commitment they put into their work, and the understanding they display of how they need to use knowledge and information, and of the support which that requires. I am convinced that the solution, if there is one, will lie in a strategy where information management, knowledge management and IT work with human beings, to support them in managing what they know, by growing, exchanging, transforming, creating and applying knowledge to drive the organization in the appropriate direction.

The visual metaphor that has come from recent work with organizations, and from discussions with colleagues over interpreting findings and recommending action, is something like a helix, a spiral, or a turbine, as shown in Figure 7.6, (*see* p145) where continuous forward movement is driven by intertwined, interacting knowledge and information, managed by the combination of human minds and technology, and powered by the energy that comes from transforming information to knowledge and knowledge to information.

The domains of KM and IM

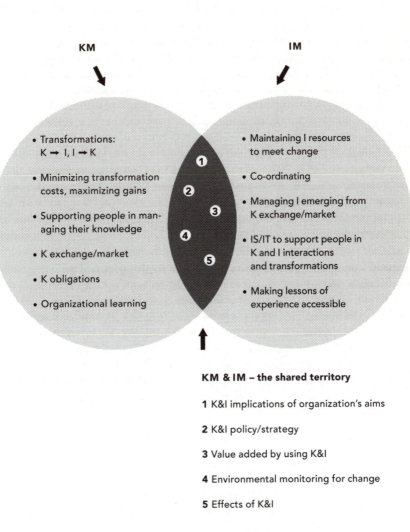

KM

IM

- Transformations:
  K → I, I → K

- Minimizing transformation
  costs, maximizing gains

- Supporting people in managing their knowledge

- K exchange/market

- K obligations

- Organizational learning

① ② ③ ④ ⑤

- Maintaining I resources
  to meet change

- Co-ordinating

- Managing I emerging from
  K exchange/market

- IS/IT to support people in
  K and I interactions
  and transformations

- Making lessons of
  experience accessible

KM & IM – the shared territory

1 K&I implications of organization's aims

2 K&I policy/strategy

3 Value added by using K&I

4 Environmental monitoring for change

5 Effects of K&I

Figure 7.5
The domains and shared terrritory of knowledge
management and information management

I visualize that going on in all areas, at all levels and in every business process, applied strategically in different ways in different areas and situations:

● To embodying learning in the knowledge base, and so 'enhancing capability to cope with similar situations' as Menou (1998) puts it ● To keeping complexity from tipping over the edge into chaos, allowing innovation and value to be gained from freedom and wide-ranging thinking ● To promoting order and standards where they are needed, but without letting them harden into constraints that stop forward movement – a process that Boisot (1998) describes as '... navigating at the edge of chaos' between excessive complexity and excessive order, steering productive activity 'now towards complexity reduction and now towards complexity absorption'.

The lessons for strategy development are:

Lesson

● Recognize the need for both information management and knowledge management, and their mutual interdependence ● Provide resources for both, and encourage constant interaction between them ● Establish an integrated group to oversee the management of knowledge and information in the organization and monitor the outcomes ● Feed the results of monitoring into developing the organization's business strategy.

Summary – what information and knowledge strategy should do for organizations

Now it is time to bring together the lessons for information and knowledge strategy drawn from the themes and arguments of this chapter. They do not in themselves make a strategy, but they do represent the strategic issues that any organization serious about developing an information strategy will need to formulate in terms relevant to its own activities, aspirations and culture – though preferably not all at one go! I still strongly recommend the spiral of 'Develop–implement–learn' described in Chapter 6 (pp109, 111).

Lesson

● Keep the organization's definitions of essential knowledge and information in line with what it seeks to do ● Ensure that it has appropriate 'tools of the mind' for setting and maintaining standards, and that people are able to use them, with full support from the technology ● Balance investment in technology with appropriate investment in supporting human interactions ● Value human minds and reward thinking ● Support and reward reciprocal information responsibility ● Monitor how people use information and knowledge in the organization's work ● Record the results of initiatives and make them accessible ● Collect examples of value added by information orientation, of risks from which it has saved the organization, and of failures and errors that could have been avoided by better use of information ● Use the lessons in forward planning for future business value ● Give thinking time to understanding the organization's own culture, and to working out strategies for feasible changes ● Provide resources of finance and skill for environmental sensing, for bringing the results of it into organizational consciousness and knowledge, and for managing the relevant information content ● Recognize the need for both information management and knowledge management, and their mutual interdependence ● Provide resources for both,

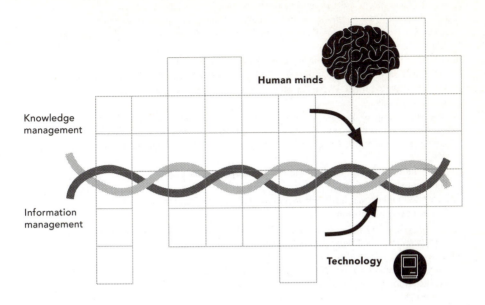

Figure 7.6
The interaction of knowledge and information,
managed by human minds and technology, and
powered by transforming K,I and I,K

and encourage constant interaction between them ● Establish an integrated group to oversee the management of knowledge and information in the organization and monitor the outcomes ● Feed the results of monitoring into developing the organization's business strategy.

References

BEARD, A., GRANT, S., HOUGHTON, B., AND NAIRNE, S. (2001), 'Towards a broader strategy', *Museum Documentation Association Annual report 1999/2000*, 12–15.

BOISOT, M. (1998), *Knowledge Assets. Securing competitive advantage in the knowledge economy*, Oxford: Oxford University Press.

CHECKLAND, P. and HOLWELL, S. (1998), *Information, Systems and Information Systems: making sense of the field*, Chichester: John Wiley and Sons.

CHECKLAND, P. and SCHOLES, J. (original edition 1990; reprinted 1999 with a '30-y retrospective'), *Soft systems methodology in action*, Chichester: John Wiley.

CLARKE, P. (2001), 'Knowledge Toolkits from Verity', *Knowledge Management*, April 2001.

COHEN, D. and PRUSAK, L. (2001), *In good company: how social capital makes organizations work*, Boston, MA: Harvard Business School Press.

COLLINS, T. with BICKNELL, D. (1997), *Crash. Learning from the world's worst computer disasters*, London: Simon & Schuster.

DAVENPORT, T. H. and PRUSAK, L. (1998), *Working Knowledge*, Boston, MA: Harvard Business School Press.

DRUCKER, P. (1995), *Managing in a Time of Great Change*, Oxford: Butterworth Heinemann.

... (1999), *Management Challenges for the 21st century*, New York: Harperbusiness.

EDOLS, L. (2001),'Taxonomies are what?' Freepint, 04 10 01, http://www.freepint.com.

GOULD, S. J. (2002), 'When fossils were young', *I have landed; splashes and reflections in natural history*, London: Jonathan Cape.

GRAEF, J. (2002), Montague Institute, http://www.montague.com.

HYAMS. E. (2002), 'All change at the DTI', *LIBRARY + INFORMATION update*, 1 (9) 47–48.

ITAMI, H. with ROEHL, T. W., (1987), *Mobilizing Invisible Assets*, Boston, MA: Harvard University Press.

MCARTHUR, T. (1986), *Worlds of Reference*, Cambridge: Cambridge University Press.

MARCHAND, D., KETTINGER, W. and ROLLINS, J (2001), *Making the invisible visible. How companies win with the right information, people and IT*, Chichester: John Wiley & Sons Ltd.

... (2002), *Information Orientation. The link to business performance*, Oxford: Oxford University Press.

MENOU, M. (1998), 'Does information make any difference?' British Library RIC *Research Bulletin*, Autumn, 10–12.

NONAKA, P. and TAKEUCHI, M. (1995), *The Knowledge-creating Company: how Japanese companies create the dynamics of information*, New York: Oxford University Press.

OPPENHEIM, C., STENSON, J., and WILSON, R. M. S. (2002a), 'A new approach to valuing information assets', *Proceedings of the 26th Online Information Conference*, Oxford: Learned Information, pp21–31.

... (2002b) *The attributes of information as an asset, its measurement and role in enhancing organisational effectiveness*. Unpublished Report to AHRB.

ORNA, E. (1996), 'Valuing information: problems and opportunities', In D. Best (ed) *The Fourth Resource: information and its management*, Aldershot: Aslib/Gower.

... (1999) *Practical Information Policies*, Ed2, pp138–151, Aldershot: Gower.

... (2000a), 'People and technology: battlefield or creative interaction?', *Law Librarian*, 31 (3) 132–140.

... (2000b), 'The human face of information auditing', *Managing Information*, 7 (4) 40–42.

STIBIC, V. (1980), *Personal Documentation for professionals*, Amsterdam: North-Holland

Other reading

BAILEY, C. and CLARKE, M. (2000),'How do managers use knowledge about knowledge management', *Journal of Knowledge Management*, 4 (3) 235–243.

Surveys show that managers have difficulty in conceptualizing knowledge. Authors propose a framework for understanding KMthat managers can use as the basis of an audit to assess their KM environment.

BLACK, A. and BRUNT, R. (2000), 'M15 1909–1945: an information management perspective', *Journal of Information Science*, 26 (3) 185–197.

Instructive tale, with applications for today, which shows from recently declassified documents that 'the formal recognition of the value of information management in organizations occurred well before the onset of the computer age'– before and during the First World War. Suggests that collapse of the MI5 system in the interwar years was caused by 'inward-looking culture' reluctant to look 'outside the organisation to con temporary practice in business and library.science.'

CLARKE, P. (2002), 'Knowledge toolkits from Verity', *Knowledge Management*, April, 34–36.

Account of the use of Verity for KM support at a consultancy firm, to help consultants navigate through all the content on an intranet. Combination of automated and human activity; each project in the firm has a human knowledge co-ordinator, responsible for capturing knowledge and for learning aspects.

DALE, A. (2001), 'Dispatches: Letters from the Corporanian war zone. Letter 6 –Information sorties and skirmishes in the public sector.', *Journal of Information Science*, 27 (5) 351–354.

Stories of the gaps between 'policy words from the top' about e-government and what happens on the ground, where 'there seems to be no one translating these ideas into practical information policy.' (For an update from information professionals working on different areas of developing e-government, which shows some awareness of all that needs to be done to make it work, see the series of articles in: *LIBRARY+INFORMATION update*, 1 (3), pp39–55).

DETLOR, B. (2000),'The corporate portal as information infrastructure: towards a framework for portal design', *International Journal of Information Management*, 20, 91–101.

Good sense about corporate portals as 'shared information work space' that can help users make better sense of the information they receive, allow them to 'engage in conver sations and negotiations with others in the firm so that shared interpretations can be made', and help them manage information flow. Draws on Taylor's value-added model and Davenport's 'information ecology' (Taylor, R. S. 1986, *Value-added processes in informa tion systems,* Norwood: Ablex Publishing, N. J. Davenport, T. H, 1997, *Information ecology.* New York:Oxford University Press).

GILCHRIST, A. (2001), 'Corporate taxonomies: report on a survey of current practice', *Online Information Review*, 15 (2) 94–102.

A TFPL survey, with six detailed cases and 16 shorter ones; the organizations surveyed were prepared to invest a lot of human resources, as well as using software in new and imaginative ways. Conclusions: over-reliance on software solutions is dangerous; multi-disciplinary teamwork and user participation are necessary.

MARTIN, W. J. (2000), 'Approaches to the measurement of the impact of knowledge manage ment programmes', *Journal of Information Science*, 26 (1) 21–27.

Useful review of intellectual capital measurement techniques, linking KM and the value of intangibles. Survey of major companies in US and Canada on implementing measures of intangbles: indicates that while managers realize that a range of non-financial factors have impact on organizational performance, they aren't sure what to do with this information. Concludes that if businesses want to use measurement of intangibles, they need a clear understanding of their strategic objectives and business processes.

MACASKILL, C. (2002), 'How to recession-proof your organisation', *Knowledge Management*, Dec/Jan 18–20.

Sensible advice on using knowledge to cope with change in the economic environment. Recommendations include: knowledge audit; review of communication channels; analysis of business processes that cross functional boundaries; standardizing key documentation and ensuring that all have access to current version; formalized 'After Action Review' process to learn from success/failure. 'It is the responsibility of senior management to lead by example in documenting and disseminating information of worth to the organisation.'

McCRACKEN, C. (2001) 'Communication breakdown', *Knowledge Management*, Feb, 18–23.

Covers access to tacit information via employee to employee exchange; capturing content in electronic environment. Virtual communities need to provide incentives for participation – it has to be easy for people to contribute knowledge. Examples of products to support communities and communication, allowing content-quality monitoring by human experts.

NEWMAN, V. (2002), 'Intellectual capital: trick or treat', *Knowledge Management*, Dec/Jan 24–25.

Argues that 'the most significant proportion of the Intellectual Capital balance is human capital the potential value of the aggregated capabilities of individuals to create and renew market value.' The primary weakness of intellectual capital thinking 'lies in the assertion that knowledge and those assets that create and distribute knowledge can be managed just like physical assets'.

Practical advice on dealing with problems on the way

8.

This final chapter returns to the strictly down to earth, with some experience-based advice which I hope will be useful to all readers, but perhaps especially to those at the start of their career as information professionals. Anyone trying to carry through the processes described in the earlier chapters, and involved in taking action on the outcomes, is likely to encounter problems and challenges – usually in the form of people. It can be a painful experience, especially the first time around, but if you're prepared to see it as an integral part of organizational life, it can be a great opportunity for developing social and tactical skills, and not without entertaining aspects. And it's not all battles; there can also be fruitful negotiations, allies found in unexpected quarters, arrivals at mutual understandings, and, sometimes, victories over potential foes which are won off the field, without them realizing what has happened till it's too late for them to do anything about it.

Story

A true story to illustrate that last point:

My first information audit was done as a direct consequence of 'tribal behaviour' in the organization where I was responsible for the library and information service.

It happened like this: the organization had called in external management consultants to look at the whole range of its activities, and two members of its staff were attached to the team – both from the same colonial civil service background. Came the turn of the information service, and our exchanges with the consultancy team were friendly and businesslike; they had no difficulty in understanding what we did. Afterwards, Mr L, one of the two internal members, started hanging around the library and making himself affable (even to the extent of kissing the librarian's hand), and putting odd requests for information.

Next, we learned from a colleague running the information service in a sister organization that Mr L had been to visit her, anxious to learn about their work because, as he confided, he would shortly be managing a similar department in our organization. We awaited his next visit to us with interest; when he arrived, my colleague the librarian welcomed him with the gracious aplomb which was her special gift, 'Ah, Brian,' she said, 'I'm so glad you've been to see Diana; you couldn't go to a better person for advice on running an information service.' He turned various colours, and, as the police reports used to say, made an excuse and left. We told our line manager that we had reason to believe a takeover plot was afoot; she was a little incredulous, but within a few days the consultants presented an interim report to the senior management team, of which she was a member, recommending that Mr L should take over the management of the information service. Our manager was noted for hitting the ceiling when the occasion required, and she did it then. It quickly emerged that there were no grounds in the quality of the service recommending a change of management;

the proposal was the discreditable fruit of a conspiracy to get Mr L a higher-status job than that of O&M manager, which he was currently gracing.

The upshot was enjoyable, at any rate for some of us; the Director of the organization asked me to chair a working group (Mr L was a very quiet member of it) with the task of looking at what collections of information there were in different parts of the organization and how information flowed between them, and defining the role of the information service. In effect, an information audit. It led to new and productive information interactions, and a clear agreement with management about the respective roles of the information service and of other functions that collected and managed information. A useful experience, and a lesson in how to turn to good advantage the varied manifestations of human nature that flourish in all organizations.

Upward interactions

Information managers can help themselves and the organization by building good relations with well-chosen management sponsors as their regular bridge to the top of the organization (obviously including their line manager, but it needn't be restricted to that; the nature of the information manager's job gives sanction and scope for building understanding with other potential sponsors). Management sponsors should be gently educated as apostles for information issues, and fed a regular strategic diet of carefully presented relevant ideas, which they can make their own and sell on to their colleagues.

The aim is to help decision makers to understand the true nature of the professional knowledge and skills which information managers are paid to exercise. If you concentrate on building trust in your reliability and good sense over time (it does take time, but it's worth it), you will stand a good chance of being able to get on with doing what the organization pays you to do, subject to sensible reporting and control arrangements (which you help to design); and it will be established that this is the territory which you are responsible for developing on behalf of the organization, that you have authority within it, and a recognized stake in any proposed changes. And information managers who set a just value on their own professional abilities and knowledge, and are ready to stand up and argue for them, are most likely to convince management of their value.

In making a business case for any information initiative it is important to use both what the organization says officially about itself in its 'mission statement', 'vision' or corporate objectives (because it can hardly repudiate them as a basis for argument), and understanding of its parallel world of organizational politics and power relations. Davenport's (1992) analysis of the different models of organizational politics, from feudal to federal via anarchy and monarchy, has been quoted in Chapter 6 (p105). He also points out that 'The key in managing information politics is to know which political model is currently in ascendance within the firm and to which the organization should be moving' (p62), and that all kinds of organizational changes require changed information policies if the organization is to benefit from them. So information managers should always be alert and ready to take advantage of all kinds of organizational change to sell appropriate information strategies to go with it.

Interactions around the organization

It is the responsibility of those who manage information as their main job, or as part of another job, to take initiatives in meeting the relevant stakeholders, especially those with whom they need to exchange information, and talking about information issues on an equal footing. It can be done either informally, or, if necessary, with an impartial 'referee' to insist on clear and non-adversarial explanations and negotiations – either way, the agreed outcome needs to be recorded for future reference. This is the only way to clear misconceptions and produce better understanding. It has to be a real exchange, in which everyone respects the participants' knowledge and judgements of their own experience in using knowledge and information in their work, and is able to explain what they do, why they do it, and the problems they experience. The best outcome is cross-boundary alliances with colleagues who might otherwise be potential rivals or enemies

Potential spoilers, allies for projects

An important part of planning for information projects is spotting, on the one hand:
- People who are potential underminers • Those who may consider their work, perceptions of status, etc, will be adversely affected by the outcome, and on the other:
- Those who are likely to see benefits to themselves from success of the project
- Other 'information-aware' potential supporters • Those who have valuable knowledge to contribute • Related projects which will be affected by this one, and the people responsible for them (often overlooked in planning, and as a result transformed into obstacles instead of allies).

Once identified, it's possible to plan strategies for getting the best from each situation. If you are managing a project such as an information audit, it's important to take the lead in negotiating solutions that will help all parties, and to deal directly wherever possible – apart from building good relations, it establishes your authority in the matter. Where the political or power situation makes that impossible, it's wise to avoid a direct run-in which would be harmful to the project, and personally. The best solution is to use your management sponsors to neutralize potential damage; in one organization where I worked, the instructions for this procedure were 'prime Mrs V, point her in the right direction, light blue touch paper, and retire at once'.

Story

An information audit was being run by an in-house team with consultancy support. The project manager found his work was under direct and indirect email attack from a senior member in one department, casting doubt upon the competence of the audit team and the group to which it belonged. The source was a key stakeholder representative of her department, who had to be interviewed during the audit. The project manager decided to use the consultant for that interview, to avoid direct confrontation, and to ensure a positive result from the interview. The discussion went well; the stakeholder contributed very useful observations from her particular background of knowledge, but she also revealed deep mistrust and misconceptions about the group of in-house information professionals running the audit. She believed, inaccurately, that they were technology-obsessed specialists without understanding of the nature and history of the organization. After the interview, she continued gunning for the project manager via email, on the basis of the draft report about the audit of her department. It was only when senior managers from her department and from the one with overall responsibility for the audit were able to meet with the project manager and consultant that the situation was understood and the potential damage to the audit could be neutralized. A lot of trouble would have been avoided if that discussion had taken place immediately after the interview.

If you're a newcomer

Beginning a new job as an information manager, particularly if it is your first, can be a time of apprehension as well as exhilaration. The main thing to remember: it takes time to be recognized and listened to, and respect has to be won by showing competence, perseverance and goodwill. Time given to learning about the organization, from what it says officially about itself, from colleagues, from observation of what it does, and to thinking about what all that means in terms of what it should be doing with knowledge and information, is time well spent. So too is finding out about the expected norms of behaviour and how to observe them so that you are seen as someone who knows how to behave – especially by those in other functions (particularly Personnel – or 'Anti-personnel' as it is known in some establishments) who are well established rather further up the hierarchy and have some power to affect what you do. A little effort devoted to feeding the organizational machine with the 'right' responses is likely be repaid in terms of a lot more freedom to get on with your job without unnecessary interference. More positively, it is worth seeking 'mentors' among knowledgeable colleagues, for whatever informal education they can give, as well as taking every opportunity for more formal training about the job and the organization. All that should put you in a good position to spot any information territory that needs developing, and to win the right to take it on as your 'allotment' and cultivate it.

Working with information consultants

This can be a pretty gruesome experience, or a positive and enjoyable one. There are two distinct possible roles for consultants, which should not be confused:
1 They are hired to do all the work to a specific brief
2 They are required to provide support, advice and/or training for an in-house team who will do the main work – what might be called 'collaborative consultancy'.
In both cases the organization should ensure these essentials:
● A clear initial brief, drawn up by the organization (with participation by information professionals); this becomes the basis for discussion, proposals from consultants and decisions on them, and for final agreed terms of reference for the assignment ● A clear definition of how the project will be managed: who will have responsibility on the in-house side for co-ordination, who the consultants will report to, at what stages, what the 'deliverables' from it will be.

It is the responsibility of the commissioning organization, and in particular of whoever it makes responsible for the project (preferably a senior information professional), to get everyone concerned signed up to the necessary documents, as a basis for monitoring what happens, and ensuring that agreed actions have been taken, and deliverables actually handed over.

If consultants are hired to carry through the whole project, it is particularly important to ensure authoritative in-house project management, at an appropriately senior level, and involving key stakeholders and people with relevant knowledge as a steering committee which receives regular reports and gives advice on any problems as they arise. Where those conditions are not met, conscientious and highly competent work by consultants, with positive co-operation and high expectations from in-house staff, can be undermined and fail to give the potential benefits – because there are no appropriate intermediaries to promote proper communication between them and senior management (the report described in Chapter 4 Part 2, p83, was an element in a situation like this – had there been proper in-house management of the assignment, that specific problem would never have arisen, and the outcome from the consultants' work would have been more beneficial to the organization).

If the project is to be run in-house, with consultancy support, the important message is mutual respect, and commitment by both sides to progressive learning and take-over of responsibility by the in-house team. This kind of consultancy is potentially very rewarding for both parties, but it needs very careful management from the start.

Story A consultancy team was commissioned by an organization to train an in-house group, led by the organization's information manager, with his manager as project sponsor, and to support them in carrying through an information audit. There was a great deal of goodwill and determination to get it right on both sides – perhaps a bit too much of the latter on the side of the consultants. The in-house team were all well-qualified in their own specialisms, young, and anxious to learn and to exercise what they had learned. As the project progressed, perhaps because it was being done to a very tight timetable, the team came to feel that the consultants weren't trusting them to work on their own; they recognized the consultants' anxiety to be seen as earning their keep by delivering the goods, but felt undermined and disappointed that they were not allowed to develop new and valuable skills and apply their knowledge of the organization in new ways that would benefit both the organization and their own careers. There was a distinct feeling that the 'grown-ups' were doing all the important things.

Lessons from that experience were applied in recent work in another organization; there was clear agreement at the start about the division of work between outside and in-house, the time schedule allowed for progressive handover, and it was an acknowledged part of the assignment to give training and development in information auditing skills. A reasonable timetable, with just the right amount of pressure, and an excellent in-house project manager, made possible good informal, but efficient, collaboration, in which the consultant contributed specialist skills and experience-based advice while the project manager applied knowledge of the organization, understanding of its politics and inter-personal skills to good effect.

Information management responsibilities without being an information professional

Many people who are not information professionals have, as part of their job, some information management responsibilities, which are incidental, rather than central to it. For many of them, the information-management element in their work is not recognized by the organization, and no training is available. If that is your situation, then the first step should be to consult whoever is responsible for professional information management, with a view to identifying everyone in the organization who has incidental information management as part of the job. Then everyone concerned should get together to explain their information-management responsibilities, and with the help of the information professionals identify the core training that they all need, together with any specific elements. Armed with that, they can then talk to training staff about the most appropriate way of providing it as part of the organization's overall training plan. This process will probably show common needs for help with basic techniques of information content management, and reveal that many people need more help than is currently given in using the available technology. It will also be very useful to professional information managers in revealing where, in the absence of standard procedures, people have been driven to invent their own; they can then plan to establish proper organization-wide standards.

An initiative like this can lead to a regular forum for 'incidental information managers', together with the information professionals in information systems/IT as well as information management. That in turn can help them to make sure of being heard as stakeholders in any audit or information strategy projects. Besides appropriate training, the agenda should also include:
● Job descriptions that describe the information responsibilities and exchanges required of job holders (*see* Chapter 7, p130) ● Standards for information management activities and procedures ● Recognition of incidental information management as a job element in performance assessment.

Managing information managers without being an information professional

Many managers with other professional backgrounds find themselves responsible for the work of professional information managers. I have observed that many of them are at something of a loss as to what they should expect of the information professionals they manage, and that the lack of knowledge leads more often to under- than over-estimation. That can mean that the organization fails to get the benefit it should from their professional abilities, and that they, aware of the lack of opportunity for exercising them, seek better chances of career development elsewhere.

It is always a difficult situation to find yourself responsible for areas of work of which, for good reason, you have no in-depth knowledge; and other demands of the job can make it difficult to find time to learn more. Readers who are in that situation could none the less find benefit from setting up some occasions for knowledge exchange with information managers and other key stakeholders in the use of information. The agenda could profitably include:

- Defining what knowledge and information are essential for the organization, in the light of what it aims to achieve – the views of information managers, and your comments from the standpoint of your role and your knowledge of the organization
- Explanations by the participants of their respective professional knowledge and skills, and questioning to help arrive at a good mutual understanding and agreement about how best they can be applied to meet team, departmental and organizational objectives
- Identifying discrepancies between what the information managers are capable of contributing and what they are currently asked to do, and then making sure that the top of the organization reflects on the findings and takes action to remedy any wasted opportunities.

An organization that had committed itself to knowledge management set up an information audit as a first step. The project manager of the in-house audit team was an information professional who had for some time been managing the organization's library and information service. As the audit looked at the organization's information environment, it became apparent that senior management had a remarkably limited understanding of the role of information management, of its relation to knowledge management, and of the capabilities of information professionals. Until the audit gave her the opportunity to emerge from the background, the information manager's contacts with senior managers had been limited to an annual discussion at budget time of the books each of them wished the library to acquire for them.

There are of course obligations on both sides in these matters, and it is incumbent on information professionals, as a matter of courtesy as well as self-interest, to invite their managers into their world, make them welcome, learn from them, and build the bridges of understanding that are essential for developing a strong information strategy.

Making sure that investment in strategy development isn't wasted

This final section is on a very important subject, and is relevant for all readers. Experience of organizations shows that they often get poor returns on investments in doing things with information. IT investment is the most notorious case, but it happens time and again on a smaller scale with initiatives that are intended to lead to more profitable use of information content. There are a number of characteristic ways in which this kind of investment of time, finance and effort can be wasted:
- Change at the top of the organization (which can of course have a positive as well as a negative effect)
- Loss of sponsor
- External pressure on the top of the organization in the form of: o financial imperatives o the general economic climate o specific market conditions o external changes that require new initiatives to comply with them (on the part of private businesses as well as government and public organizations) o New 'fads' or buzzwords that are being overhyped without being fully understood by the decision-makers at whom they are aimed o Simple forgetting, or organizational oblivion – which may be the most common cause.

These threats to getting value from information initiatives, and safeguards against them, are discussed below.

Detrimental change at the top

This is typically brought about by the arrival of new incumbents who have no interest in information, and other priorities to pursue. Sponsors and allies can be useful for advance warning of risks of this kind, and can help protect against them. The best way to insure against the worst effects of a change at the top while an information project is in progress is to concentrate on making useful changes that don't prejudice the main outcome in the course of the project, without waiting for the end and for senior management agreement to them as recommendations. In that way, the beneficial changes can become part of the fabric of what people do, seen as by them as actually useful and not subject to question.

As advised earlier (see pp89–92), it is always wise to present just the essential minimum for top-level decisions. Remember you have the best chance of agreement if you're asking for in-principle assent to get on with doing things, rather than seeking top-level decisions on detailed recommendations. Once it's handed back down to you, it's work in progress and you should be able to get on with it quietly without attracting attention. If that can't be done, and as often happens, an information project, like many other things in progress, is put on hold, don't let it slide into oblivion; make sure what has been done is properly recorded ready for moving on, watch for opportunities to revive it, and keep it to the fore with those to whom you are responsible. Large projects that haven't got properly started are in particular danger – if they get put on ice, take it as an opportunity to refine the thinking, prepare the ground some more, and wait for better times, which may well come; keep an eye open for opportunities and get in smartly if they occur. The worst losses are initiatives that have gone right through but without adequate protection (a story of one such case – at NatWest Markets – is told in Orna, 1999, p295 et seq), and are then lost in entirety when their sponsor is no longer there to protect them. It's wise to try to safeguard against that at the start, by making sure of the durability of support at the top; this is another situation where piloting reduces risk and gives a chance of yielding something useful that can be returned to in more favourable circumstances.

External pressures and new fads

Watch out for these on the horizon by 'sensing' the environment; use networks and knowledgeable contacts to the full for identifying significant issues. When you identify a potential threat of this kind, think ahead about how it can be turned to advantage – how a case for doing something about knowledge and information can be hooked on to whatever is the New Thing; prepare arguments to show that the New Thing can't be achieved without the information initiative, and to show the benefits it can bring and the threats it could help avoid.[1]

1 Davenport et al (1992) point out in the article quoted earlier (p62) that when organizations are forced by external events into changes like restructuring, they often realize after successfully weathering the changes that they could not have done so without new policies for information.

This kind of action can be linked with the regular feeding of management sponsors with information about important changes in the environment, so that they are well informed about both the subject and the opportunity it offers for information initiatives.

Organizational oblivion

Those who go into organizations to help them with information initiatives often meet staff members who have long experience there and long memories to go with it, which have bred a degree of cynicism in them. Their accounts of comparable earlier initiatives and what became of them are worth listening to with respect, because there are lessons for the present in them. A fate frequently reported is on the lines – management requested an investigation of such and such, we did it, and prepared a report with recommendations, it was taken up into the heavens and seen no more, and we never did hear what became of it. The responsibility for this kind of situation lies on both sides; if the top of the organization is in the habit of requesting information but not of responding to it, the onus is on the people who fulfil those requests to consider their job is not done until they have elicited a response, and not to let it go by default. If they let it go from a conviction that nothing will ever change, and they have better things to do with their time, even though that is understandable, they have done less than they should for their own professional satisfaction, and for the good of the organization.

If your organization is prone to this brand of high-level amnesia, it is particularly important to use formal procedures for initiating projects, agreeing terms of reference, reporting arrangements and monitoring and evaluation criteria, and to be punctilious in following them through at every stage, using management sponsors for all they are worth to make sure that top management's memory is prompted, and that it keeps to the obligations it has set in train.

Make sure that every stage of the progress of any information project is documented, input, and indexed, especially the final report, presentations, and decisions – as a model for what should happen for all projects. Publicize the project and its progress through the in-house media – intranet, in-house newsletters, etc; use allies who have taken part in it to help spread knowledge among their colleagues. All this activity, which is a legitimate obligation on information managers, can make it much harder for organizational oblivion to overtake valuable information projects.

Looking back over these final words that I have just written I think they reflect the message of the whole of this book; it is the right and the duty of professional information managers to be active initiative-takers and bridge builders in their organizations; it is the only way to make sure that their unique but little understood kind of knowledge can work fully to the benefit of their organizations.

References
DAVENPORT, T. H., ECCLES, R. G. and PRUSAK, L. (1992), 'Information politics',
    Sloan Management Review, Fall, 53–65.
ORNA, E. (1999), *Practical Information Policies*, Ed2, Aldershot: Gower.

Index

continued